Pleasure

AN ALMANAC
FOR THE HEART

NIKKI GEMMELL

illustrations by PAULA SANZ CABALLERO

FOURTH ESTATE • *London, New York, Sydney and Auckland*

'I like not only to be loved, but also to be told
that I am loved. I am not sure that you are
of the same kind. But the realm of silence is
large enough beyond the grave. This is the
world of light and speech, and I shall take
leave to tell you that you are very dear.'

GEORGE ELIOT — LETTER TO A FRIEND

Fourth Estate
An imprint of HarperCollins*Publishers*

First published in Australia in 2006
by HarperCollins*Publishers* Australia Pty Limited
ABN 36 009 913 517
www.harpercollins.com.au

Published in the United Kingdom in 2006,
by Fourth Estate, an imprint of HarperCollins*Publishers*.
www.4thestate.co.uk

HarperCollins*Publishers*
25 Ryde Road, Pymble, Sydney, NSW 2073, Australia
31 View Road, Glenfield, Auckland 10, New Zealand
77–85 Fulham Palace Road, London, W6 8JB, United Kingdom
2 Bloor Street East, 20th floor, Toronto, Ontario M4W 1A8, Canada
10 East 53rd Street, New York NY 10022, USA

National Library of Australia Cataloguing-in-Publication data:

Gemmell, Nikki.
    Pleasure : an almanac for the heart.
    1st ed.
    ISBN 9780732284404.
    ISBN 0 7322 8440 6.
    1. Women - Anecdotes.
    2. Femininity - Anecdotes. I. Title.
305.4

ISBN (UK) 0 00 72 4620 X
ISBN-13 (UK) 978 0 00 724620 5
A catalogue record for this book is available from the British Library.

Cover and internal design by Natalie Winter
Typeset in Charter 9.5/14 by Natalie Winter
Printed and bound in Australia by Griffin Press on 80gsm Belle.

5 4 3 2 1   06 07 08 09

For Elayn,
who teaches me so much

TABLE OF CONTENTS

One

LESSONS LEARNT THE HARD WAY

(IT'S BEEN A LONG JOURNEY)

ise action...

The only true failure is in not doing anything.

❧

Everyone you come across — be they heart-liftingly good or sour of spirit — is your teacher in some way. How are you growing from the experience of knowing them? How are they teaching you to become a better person?

❧

Respect someone else's dreams. For dreams are important, spirit-filled, a beacon; they give someone the gift of purpose and a fire in their belly. The crushing of spirit is a crime against what it means — gloriously — to be human.

❧

Courage isn't needed so much for the shocking, shattering blow — but for that long, lonely, rocky cliff you'll need to climb, to haul yourself back into peacefulness.

*Cultivate friends for what is in their heart.
Not for how they look. Or what they do.
Or what they can do for you.*

∞

*Our lives are made rich by reaching out to others,
not by surrounding ourselves with a boundary of 'no'.*

∞

*Never forget that a gentleman, or lady,
always does the kind thing.*

∞

*We always know how to act with goodness,
but whether we choose to heed our inner voice is
another matter. We should. For serenity's sake.*

∞

*The question should always be asked —
is this the right thing to do?*

Change is a gift. It's moving us forwards, always.

∞

*Failure humbles us, which is no bad thing.
Learn to laugh at the gift of it.*

∞

*Never forget the power in forgiveness.
It can be incredibly releasing — it can flush you clean,
uplift you, move you on.*

∞

*The lows will pass. They come into our life for a
reason — to enrich us, to draw us closer into the vast,
glittery vividness of what it is to be human. Pain softens
our hard edges and deepens our interaction with others.
It helps us learn so that we can then venture into the
world wiser, softer, richer, more compassionate. It is all
part of a bigger picture; a scarred, complex, intricate,
glorious map of our living.*

*We can crack open our life to love by the simple
action of giving it. Being loving invites love to us.*

∞

*Remember that the sudden decision to stop fighting, and
just go with the flow, can be incredibly releasing. Resistance is
so draining. There is a beauty to gracious acceptance, an
energy that leads to peace. In a vexing situation try laughing
rather than snarling; try combating with a light heart.
You will ultimately be the winner — for you will have the gift
of serenity. Try letting go of the situation you cannot control,
the one that's sapping your energy and churning your sleep.
Flood your life with the relief of walking away, with dignity.*

∞

*Use your anger for something positive
and good. Don't let a situation be complicated by
your own negativity.*

∞

*Accomplishment makes us happy.
Never underestimate the power that lies in work.*

*Beware of that reducing little word 'dependent',
for it means letting ourselves be controlled by another
person, and there is a whiny unhealthiness in that.
Being dependent on someone else does not
breed contentment.*

∞

*Calm is impossible if you want to control other people, for
their will is like an eel, always slipping from your grasp. Let go.*

∞

*Shun indifference.
It is a heart-flincher, a killer of humanity.*

∞

*Impulsive behaviour is often not the best behaviour.
Thoughtful action is always preferable because it
gives us the leeway to find a better way forward. Take
a deep breath and let the right choice come to you;
listen to your inner voice. It's always seeking goodness,
happiness and peace for you.*

Doing something for someone else helps not only them but ourselves; it buoys us.

∞

The best life is an honest, caring, generous one. Goodness brings happiness.

∞

Learn to appreciate failure — and respect it. Acknowledge the courage it's taken to get that far. Seeing others strive, fail, and strive again spurs us all on. For we're witnessing the glorious, indomitable human spirit in action.

∞

Perseverance is the key.

∞

Instead of saying 'I should', say 'I will'.

In tough times, soften your face, soften your face.
Unfold it.

∞

The bad times dissolve. Always.

∞

Live with confidence and joy.
There's so much wonder and beauty in this world.
Seek it.

∞

Two

WHAT IS LOVED IN TERMS OF GIFTS, SEX, LIFE

The pleasure factor...

'If I do vow a friendship,
I'll perform it
To the last article.'

WILLIAM SHAKESPEARE

EVERYDAY ACTS OF RAVISHING KINDNESS
(THAT COST NEXT TO NOTHING)

✤ If you offer to drive a friend home in the dark — and you always should, particularly if they're a woman — wait until they're safely through the front door before driving off.

✤ Arrive on time. It shows respect. Don't be sloppy with your friendship, for eventually your friends will become sloppy with you.

✤ Don't blow friends out repeatedly. You're letting them down if you do. And within them will grow an accumulation of disappointment. They will eventually, most likely, let you go. Beware the piracy of indifference.

✤ Always, always say thank you for a gift, especially if it's been sent in the post. It lets people know that it's arrived safely.

✤ Never forget 'What can I bring?', 'How can I help?', 'What can I do?'

✤ Help with the cleaning up after a dinner party, or at least offer. One friend always insists on rinsing the dishes and it's remembered and appreciated, every time.

✤ What you put into life, you will get out of it. Kindness begets kindness.

✤ There is something so life-affirming about it, the heart-crack in the simplest of gestures.

∞

Smiling at people in supermarket lines, opening doors for them — practising those small, magnificent, spontaneous flourishes of kindness — breeds happiness. By dispensing them, we are brightening our own lives as much as anyone else's.

∞

art II

GLORIOUS ACTS OF RAVISHING KINDNESS
(FOR A FRIEND FEELING FLATTENED)

❧ When they open their front door, waggle a bunch of happy golden sunflowers around it; there is no other flower so guaranteed to spark a smile.

❧ Seize the initiative. Run a bath, light a scented candle and place a portable CD player nearby, along with a stack of magazines. Command your friend to disappear into the bathroom and not come out for a very long time.

❧ Offer to look after children for a couple of hours. Tell the mother to go away and indulge herself — and that means out of the house, completely removed from her world. Even if it's something as simple as sitting in a café and reading a magazine and dreaming. Disengagement can be tremendously therapeutic.

❧ Attack dishes in a sink.

❧ Always offer a bed to sleep on, even if it's cushions on the floor. Never deny a friend a roof over their head.

❧ Scrub the shower if you're staying at someone's place.

(Well, yes, this could be taking things a little far but a friend did it for me once, in gratitude for a stay, and I've never forgotten it.)

✤ Drop a line to a friend if you haven't heard from them for a while, a quick text or an email, especially in times of communal contact like Christmas. If a silence feels too withheld, remember that people who are hurting tend to have the desire to hibernate. They could be lying low and licking their wounds. It's often at times like these when a hand of friendship is most needed.

'I count myself in nothing else so happy
As in a soul rememb'ring my good friends.'

WILLIAM SHAKESPEARE

_P_art III

GLORIOUS ACTS OF RAVISHING KINDNESS
(FOR THE SERIOUSLY CASHED-UP)

❖ Never forget the tonic of a damn good shop. If a friend is skint, buy as a spontaneous gift a fabulous dress/scarf/bracelet they've admired.

❖ Check them into a gorgeously luxurious hotel. A girlfriend did it for me once after declaring in horror I looked every inch my age. She arranged the fairytale bliss of massages in the hotel spa, girly twin beds, room service, talk until midnight, DVDs, trashy magazines, books and sleep — blessed, restorative sleep.

❖ Send a gift voucher for a spa treatment.

❖ Organise tickets for a favourite band or play.

❖ If you come into some money, send cheques to beloved people out of the blue, with just one instruction: 'To be used for something beautiful.'

*'Noble deeds and hot baths are
the best cures for depression.'*

DODIE SMITH

GIFTS TO CHERISH

- ❖ A dinner party in honour of a friend.

- ❖ Favourite flowers.

- ❖ A tree or plant (especially, for a woman, a gardenia bush or orchid).

- ❖ A beautiful mug — it'll be in daily use, and you'll always be thought of.

- ❖ A gift voucher from a cherished shop.

- ❖ Anything that helps us to unfurl (bath oil, music, scented candle).

- ❖ A subscription to a favourite magazine.

- ❖ For a christening gift, a professional photographer for a child's portrait.

- ❖ For a big birthday (thirtieth, fortieth, fiftieth), email friends and ask them to contribute a line or two for a memory scrapbook. It costs next to nothing and will always be remembered.

'On my birthday,
he always sent my mother flowers
to thank her for having me.'

NANCY REAGAN, ON RON

Part V

MEMORABLE GIFTS IN TERMS OF SEX
(GENTLEMEN, TAKE NOTE)

- ❧ The partner who teaches a woman to be comfortable with her body.

- ❧ Better still, the partner who teaches a woman to love her body. For it will give her a sense of confidence that will relax and invigorate her, and deepen her sense of pleasure. Tell her she's beautiful.

- ❧ The man who knows what he's doing; whose touch hums; who is assured, gentle, confident.

- ❧ The man who cherishes women (surprisingly hard to find) and is not afraid of them. That love for them — and their bodies — will illuminate the whole experience.

- ❧ Kindness floors us. When a man is attentive and considerate, when he listens to what we want, we're gone. (Personally, I'm like a dog rolling over for its tummy to be tickled.)

- ❧ A sense of connecting on the deepest level; within two people, a holiness fluttering in them both.

'A man enjoys the happiness he feels, a woman
the happiness she gives.'

PIERRE CHODERLOS DE LACLOS — 'LES LIASONS DANGEREUSES'

Part VI

WHAT HOLDS THE HEART HOSTAGE
(TO SEEK WHEN DARKNESS IS VISIBLE)

- Appreciators.
- The courage in kindness.
- Hurtling into the unknown.
- The therapeutic benefits of change.
- The vivid-hearted.
- People who seem as if they've been invented by someone with an enormous imagination.
- People who overlive, not underlive.
- Grace.
- Paris.
- A partner who loves laughing in bed.
- Melodramatic skies.
- Feeling the light in your bones.
- Cathedral singing that plumes upwards, challenging the ceiling.
- A partner who's all-calming.
- Delicious, spontaneous, joyous generosity.
- Those friends, those precious few, you can completely relax with and be yourself.

Three

BODY IMAGE AND BEAUTY

T

he importance
of arousing curiosity…

'Give me beauty in the inward soul; and may the outward and the inward man be at one.'

PLATO

Part I

THE CURIOUS INCIDENT OF THE
BRAZILIAN IN THE DAY TIME

Ah, I see, so this doll-bare thing is nothing new. I read that women used tweezers in Roman times. That South Sea Islanders did it, then tattooed the bare flesh just to continue the sadomasochism. That it's a tradition in Arabic cultures.

But now, but now.

As I write, I flinch.

It's the Brazilian we're talking about.

'It makes you feel wonderfully clean,' L., my brisk New Yorker friend informs me. 'And it's the female version of Viagra. It increases sensation incredibly.'

Uh huh.

She's insisting.

She's making me feel very twentieth-century.

She's warning that I must go to a good salon that uses hard wax, not strip wax — which will remove a layer of skin.

'I had a cheap job done the first time around and it made me look like chopped liver down there. I was so raw I couldn't have sex for a month. The next time I went, I looked down and screamed. They'd made me look like Adolf Hitler.'

And I consider her a friend? I put on my reading glasses,

bury myself in a pile of books, feel very safe. (Procrastinate? Me?)

The brisk New Yorker tries again. Offers to make the appointment for me. I tell her I'm sticking to my reading. 'No, no, no! Consider it research. Take a Panadol beforehand, darling, and go first thing in the morning — so you don't have all day to obsess about it.' If only she hadn't mentioned research. Now I feel beholden. There's a gap in my knowledge that needs correcting.

I forget to take the Panadol.

Am I mad?

I am mad.

The treatment is begun by me talking (babbling?) to Carla, the beautician, a lot; to distract her from doing what she's being paid, enormously, to do. Carla informs me that women who've had children are more likely to get it done, 'because they're less shy about their bodies'. Carla informs me that her youngest client is fourteen and her eldest seventy-seven: 'She's a woman who's lived. She hasn't spent her life in front of the stove.' Carla informs me that it's time to relax, and live.

At the bracing words, every muscle in my body is clenched.

Midway through (it takes about an hour) Carla enquires if what she's doing is as painful as childbirth. 'Yes,' I gasp.

She says I'm lying. Right at this moment I am not. As she finishes up she assures me that next time will be easier. 'Next time?' I gasp. 'Oh yes,' she chirps, 'you'll want it all the time now.'

I'm not so sure.

Yes, it feels sexy, and sensation is improved. But who exactly is this excruciating practice meant to satisfy — the woman or her partner? It's fascinating that what began as a trend derived solely for male sexual fantasy (for maximum exposure, as in porn) has become a symbol of sexual empowerment for the urban female.

My husband's all for it. Until I tell him there's also an equivalent treatment for men known as 'backs, sacks and cracks'.

I recognise that look of horror on his face.

Part II

ON BEAUTY

A woman is sexy if she thinks she is.

R. always takes the difficult path. But I've watched for two decades now, and that difficult path has brought her a great richness of living and it can only be applauded. There have been wrenching lows but soaring highs and it's a vivid tapestry, in her face — the depth of the experience, the wisdom. The lightness of heart. The compassion.

D. disperses her grace. No-one seems immune from it. It seems to make everyone who comes in contact with her want to walk a little taller and straighter. As if each person has been inspired by the cleanness of her example. D. is a nun.

I've seen that intriguing serenity and strength in only two other women in my life. Both writers. All four are older women, in their fifties and sixties. And all, I think crucially, are doing exactly what they want to do in life.

The serenity of being in control. The beauty it can bring. Perhaps the serenity of the writers is also because they're filled with the creative spirit. There is such a solace in surrendering to it.

> *'...cheerfulness and content are great beautifiers,*
> *and are famous preservers of youthful looks.'*

CHARLES DICKENS

Those women who firm with a marriage proposal. Their proud, walk-tall love. How compelling is the anchoring power of marriage, still, the promise of it. Even now, in this post-feminist world. No matter how much we're taught that work should be the adventure of our lives, we're indoctrinated, as little girls, that love is. How to escape the weight and terror of that? Perhaps we can't. It is biology. That need to settle, to have a child, to nest. It is in our blood and our bones. And no amount of feminist empowerment is going to circumvent it.

I see her regularly in Starbucks. Her supermodel days are behind her but she exudes an energy, still, that is different. The energy of someone who has been gazed upon with admiration for an entire lifetime. She is the living embodiment of the power in beauty. But when I open the door for her she barely sees me; doesn't meet my eye in gratitude; sweeps through as if this kind of thankless, anonymous servitude is expected of all people around her, always. In that single moment she loses all beauty. There is none inside, for she does not connect with fellow human beings and I see her, suddenly, husked.

Excessive dieting reduces the sex drive. Excessive dieting is all about control. Is it any wonder that women who diet to the extreme lose their taste for sex, that one time in life when the aim is surrender, a letting go?

J. declared, joyously, that the best sex she'd ever had was after she started putting on weight. Because she felt womanly and horny and greedy for it. For the first time in her life.

'At age fifty, every man has the face he deserves.'

GEORGE ORWELL

V.'s fifty-something face is remarkably unlined, reflecting the person she is — a good person. Joyous, quick to forgive, easy to move on. She never holds grudges tight within her; never allows a festering. She knows the power of forgiveness, the cleansing, rejuvenating energy it releases. It frees her.

The idea of owning your beauty — can only older people do that? Julie Christie, now, as opposed to younger. A face trapping the inner beauty of experience; a face that's lived, fully and richly. When she was younger, it wasn't quite owned. It was like a brand new house that needed the marks of living within it to make it a home.

The horror of finding the passport photo from my early twenties. Caked in makeup, masked. Gradually I stopped wearing so much — living in the desert beat it out of me. And I ended up looking younger at thirty than I did at twenty.

Why do I always suspect that people wearing perfume are covering something up?

O. talks about 'getting her face back' after so much love-sadness. It's true, her face has returned.

'Get out there and make yourself beautiful!' my aunty commands after the devastating break-up. 'Show him. Show him what he's missing out on.'

B. is freshly divorced in her late-forties. How does she fend off invisibility? 'Reinvention, my dear,' she explains, looking fifteen years younger. She's just cut all her hair and it's like she wants people to see her face again, the light in it. She's also wearing contact lenses after years of hiding behind glasses. She looks fabulous; taller and straighter. Like she finally owns her life.

She says her number one beauty secret is surrounding herself with people who make her feel good as opposed to people who flatten her in some way. 'Rid your world of the flatteners!' is her new rule. As a smug married, she says she was surrounded by them.

S. is so completely herself. She has the rare courage to live her life exactly as she wants to; she is freed from the tyranny of reputation. She doesn't care what others think. And because of that she is utterly intriguing, and in that intrigue is a fascinating beauty. It's all about confidence.

∞

Try and look gorgeous in some way every day.
Life is too fleeting not to.

∞

'There are no ugly women, only lazy ones.'

HELENA RUBENSTEIN

art III

ON UNDERNEATH

U.'s on the strawberry ice-cream side of things; me, the porridge side. Give me big, sensible, white cotton undies any day. Items that wash easily and last forever and cover all the bits.

O. has a staff of sixty. She's spent eighteen years rising to the top of her profession and spends a lot of money on underwear. Why? She answers with a flourish:

'Because...
1. It makes me feel "hot" all day, no matter how draining work/life is.
2. I love the idea of "kicking ass" with frilly knickers on.
3. It helps give me a mental edge when a male colleague's driving me crazy — you know, the old "if only he knew what I had on under this business suit" thing.
4. It reminds me I don't have balls in such a male-dominated world. Like many senior female execs, I have the tendency to take

on the dominant male characteristics of
high-poweredness. So I'm using lingerie
to salvage my own womanly sexuality,
which has been a bit thwarted in my rise
through this profession.'

Wow. The psychological power of a piece of lace.

*Beauty is about confidence of bearing.
Being comfortable in your skin. We can teach it from
a young age. Never underestimate the tonic of praise.*

Part IV

AND WHO ARE YOU?

Not only has the age been reached where I'm no longer noticed as I walk by a building site, but the age has been reached where a person leads me by the elbow as I pass through a door. It happened just this morning. Crikey, and I'm not even forty.

But you know, with the age of invisibility has come the age of relaxing. And that has meant the most satisfying sex of my life.

Because I've finally accepted who I am — and that there are some things about my body that are never going to change. So I might as well just…enjoy. The stomach's no longer sucked in as I undress for a man. Covers are no longer dived under before all the imperfections can be glimpsed. I no longer beg for the lights to be turned off. No longer angle myself during sex as if I'm viewing the scene from the ceiling and directing myself into the most flattering positions.

I was scarred early on by a lover who always checked out partners for their so-called 'fatability factor' — their ability to run to fat in old age. 'The mother's figure is always noted,' he explained. For a long time I hated the way I looked. (A tip for men: I eventually found a boyfriend who taught me to love my body. With his beautifully encouraging words I unknotted — he unlocked my sexuality. I began to enjoy making love. Before him I'd seen myself as just a catalogue of imperfections, but he cherished the female form for all its wondrous individualities and I'll never forget his spirit of generosity.)

You see, once upon a time I was a prisoner in my body, overwhelmed by its refusal to conform to the ideal of womanhood in magazines. Now — at my most imperfect — I've been freed. And lo and behold, I feel more womanly than ever. 'One of the signs of passing youth is the birth of a sense of fellowship with other human beings as we take our place among them,' Virginia Woolf wrote. And a sense of fellowship with oneself. I'm not so hard on me any more. I am no longer constantly criticising and, hallelujah, no longer seeing the body as merely a catalogue of imperfections — but as a catalogue of womanliness.

So here I am, revelling in the age of invisibility.

Because with it has come the age of confidence.

※

A light heart is wonderful armoury for living.

※

Four

IAN, A FLATMATE

The immense,
disturbing power of the
sex emotions…

'If I can stop one heart from breaking,
I shall not live in vain;
If I can ease one life the aching,
or cool one pain,
Or help one fainting robin
Unto his nest again,
I shall not live in vain.'

EMILY DICKINSON

Part I

A LOVE HAUNTING

When I was twenty-three I had a flatmate I barely knew. He was a student, eighteen, very quiet — he never really participated in the life of the house. There was another flatmate, Simon, my age. Our gentle tenant, Ian I'll call him, had just broken up traumatically with a woman of twenty-eight. He was still desperately, obsessively in love. He stayed mostly in his room.

Simon and I got on with our lives; we were starting our careers, work consumed our lives.

On the first day of spring, a Sunday, Ian drove me around his childhood haunts — home, school, his old corner shop, that kind of thing. He was chatty and buoyant, perhaps things were looking up. When we returned he went to his room. That evening he left for another drive. 'See you later,' he said as he went out the door.

The police came to us several hours afterwards. Ian had hung himself in the grounds of his girlfriend's house.

On his bed he'd left a tableau of childhood photos, music certificates and report cards. There was a note at their centre, 'I love S…forever.' His writing was like a child's.

When his father came around the next day, pale with bewilderment, I saw he knew very little about his only son and was desperate to understand. Simon and I weren't really able to help. I still feel guilty about that; that I hadn't given Ian more of my time.

For someone who'd touched my life so lightly, he's haunted it ever since. Why did he do it? Obsession, infatuation, the fire and volatility of youth, I guess. He was bound by desire, in a consumingly negative way — and in failed love can lie the weeds of mad actions and destruction.

I know. I've been there. Several years after Ian's death I almost threw myself out a window over a man I had been going to marry. It took my parents and some very good friends a long while — three years — to haul me back into optimism.

I'm much more practical about romantic love now; I'm no longer an avid fan. It's such a transient, delusional, debilitating concept. It can take possession of your life and your senses.

But usually only once. Relationships following the Big One are often shrewder, calmer, more realistic — and more healthy because of that. The lovers who embody the passion I once aspired to are Heathcliff and Cathy. In a scene in *Wuthering Heights*, where Heathcliff embraces dying Catherine — the love of his life — Emily Bronte writes that there were 'four distinct impressions left, blue in the colourless skin'. That sounds painful, and in these relationships there's a lot of pain.

Passion craves quietness, security, calm — states hard to attain in romantic love. And sometimes, as the worm turns, hurting is a way of holding someone. Suicide can be a way of hurting. Why did Ian choose to stain his lover's future so much? Isn't true love a desire for the other person's happiness?

Why did I want to do it? Among other things, to stamp my fiancé's life forever with the memory of what he'd done to me. I thought, once, there was something so passionate and brave about what Ian had done. Now I just wish he'd grown up and known other women — journeyed to a point where he could look back and laugh. I wonder, years later, if he could reflect on his actions he'd think, 'Damn it, why did I do it? For her?'

I suspect he would.

And that breaks my heart.

Five

LIVING ARRANGEMENTS

Conduct affected by
habits of the home...

'...do not be drawn away from the simplicity of your ancestors.'

MAHATMA GANDHI

INFINITE RICHES
(TO ASPIRE TO...)

A living space that has the quality of a lit candle.

Possessing with grace. And that can involve extremely simple things that have nothing to do with how much money you have: a clean white tablecloth, a grandmother's gift of a teacup, fresh flowers on the table, sunlight from clean windows.

A place of good spirit. It doesn't have to be large; it could be just a bedsit or an attic room, but a treasure trove of calm. Think of Christopher Marlowe's 'infinite riches in a little room'.

When it comes to your living space, remember what Diana Vreeland said of clothes: 'Elegance is refusal. And refusal is seductive.'

I cannot quite subscribe to it, but I'm attracted to that suggestion of ridding yourself every seven years of your possessions — or you will eventually be owned by them.

art II

MY FRIEND CHRISSY FISH'S
HOUSEHOLD HINTS FOR THE HOPELESS
(i.e. YOURS TRULY.)

❀ To avoid tears, peel onions under a running tap.

❀ Put a lid on a saucepan to make it boil quicker and save energy. (I know, this seems absolutely basic but I had to be told this one.) And while you're at it, turn down the heat slightly.

❀ Why use heavy-duty chemical cleaners in our homes? Some scientists believe that the accumulation of chemicals in our bodies is causing an increase in allergies such as asthma and eczema. Get back to basics. Bi-carb soda and warm water will clean almost anything — including the bathroom, and the kitchen.

❀ Use bread to mop up excess oil in a frying pan.

❀ Recycle your tea-bag. Use it in one mug and then another.

✤ If you only have soya milk for tea, pour it over an
  upside-down spoon — the convex side will stop the
  soya milk curdling.

✤ Wear a new rubber glove to brush fluff off dark clothes.

✤ Eucalyptus oil is the ultimate stain remover. Dab a
  little on cotton wool and sponge on the stain. (For
  dark, heavy clothes such as suits, mix the oil with
  a little water.)

✤ Eucalyptus oil also removes sticky residue left by labels.

✤ If a drawer is sticking, rub a candle or soap along
  the runners.

✤ Rub a cut lemon on a wooden chopping board to
  neutralise smells such as garlic or onion.

✤ For cut flowers, add a couple of teaspoons of sugar
  to the water — it will make them last longer. (A little
  lemonade mixed with water also does the trick.)

✤ Clean blood off your clothes by placing the item in a
  sink with no water, and let the cold tap gently run on
  the stain.

- ❧ Use newspapers to clean windows. The ink helps dissolve smears. Vinegar also cleans windows.

- ❧ Tablets used to clean dentures can also be used to clean stained china and vases. Fill with hot water, drop a tablet in and leave for half an hour.

- ❧ Wash plastic kitchenware in unscented soap and water now and then, instead of the usual detergent. They'll look cleaner.

- ❧ Invite kids to cook with you. Most love the experience, but be prepared to be patient, and listen to their ideas. My young son demanded to make chocolate pizza. I made a sweet shortcrust round base and baked it (sort of like a large biscuit). We then spread it with raspberry jam instead of tomato sauce, and added pieces of fruit — sliced peaches instead of meat, cherries instead of olives, sultanas and a bit of grated apple. Finally we dribbled melted chocolate over our ensemble and we had a chocolate pizza and very popular dessert. His next request was for ham and hundreds and thousands sandwiches. I went with the ham, but we sprinkled it with seeds — sesame, poppy, mustard etc.

❖ Wash egg from dishes in cold water before hot water, so the egg doesn't stick.

❖ To attack oil spills on concrete, sprinkle with talcum powder and rub in with a broom.

❖ To remove pen and ink marks from vinyl or toys, spray with hairspray then wipe with a dry cloth.

❖ Very fine sandpaper will clean marks off suede.

Part III

A RECIPE TO IMPRESS FOR
THE DOMESTICALLY CHALLENGED
(i.e. YOURS TRULY)

PESTO PASTA WITH TUNA AND LEMON

*Boil your pasta (spiral ones are good).
When it's ready, mix in some dollops of pesto
from a jar and a can of tuna, and squeeze a
fresh lemon through it. Add some shavings of
Parmesan. Divine and easy. Serve with a
ready-made rocket salad from the supermarket
and a fresh baguette and some lovely
crisp white wine.*

A relaxed meal — that boosts the cook's confidence
— is always preferable to a fiddly one that takes
forever to cook.

Part IV

HOME IS WHERE THE HEART BREAKS

How I'm intrigued by that tender new glow in the homes of the freshly married — the presents still in boxes, the honeymoon photos in packets, the aura of contentment in the women who've found their men. You never know, at that golden point, how the relationship will end up — if it will atrophy into indifference or weather the shock of capitulation and compromise and become a haven, a harbour, to rest from all the toss of the world.

We all have three lives: a public life, a private one and a secret one. And living together is never a guarantee that we'll get to know the person behind the mask. 'Though I spent every day with her for six years, and was rarely separated from her for more than two or three hours at a time, I never saw her show her real self to anybody,' Ted Hughes wrote in the foreword to Sylvia Plath's *Journals*.

Patrick White said living together means endless sacrifices, disappointments and patching up: 'I imagine only vegetables live happily ever after.'

You don't embark upon an enduring live-in relationship if you have to be in complete control of your universe.

R. is a man too clever to love anyone — because he knows he could never share his life with anyone. He says he recognised he was in too deep with V. when she started organising Spanish dancing classes for him.

It takes courage to embrace all the messiness of sharing your life, all the capitulation and compromise.

The strange dynamic of a man moving into a woman's home. It's emasculating for him, and requires confidence.

N. touched my place lightly, as if he knew from the start there would never be a permanence to the arrangement. Half of his belongings were still in his old place. How long did we last? Three weeks, four.

The man who had no books. Houses without books are like people without curiosity. I find them unsettling.

'How few of his friends' houses would a man choose to be at when he is sick.'

JAMES BOSWELL

'One night I dreamed that I did not love,
and that night, released from all bonds,
I lay as though in a kind of soothing death.'

COLETTE

'Wedlock — the deep, deep peace
of the double bed after the hurly-burly
of the chaise longue.'

BEATRICE (MRS PATRICK) CAMPBELL

Part V

HOLIDAYS AREN'T FOR SEX ANY MORE, THEY'RE FOR SLEEPING

Ah, shared sleep. Deeply sexy, often more so than making love. It's where true love lies; beyond words, beyond sex.

The soldering pleasure of it. D.H. Lawrence wrote: 'There are only two things now/The great black night scooped out/ And this fireglow.' Ah yes, to aspire to that. A glow in your heart that is brewed from a combination of love and quiet and security and warmth and peace.

I think it's why one of the most moving images from the film *Titanic* is of the elderly couple spooning on a bed, water swirling about them, their bodies folded together in a jigsaw fit. Why is that brief moment so wrenching? Because it encapsulates the infinitely tender and deeply comforting bond that can be found in sleeping beside someone beloved.

M. is a high-powered career woman. She could never sleep with a man beside her because of the trust in it, the relaxing. She was tight and controlled; everything had to be just so. She'd never had an orgasm, had never worked out how to let go. At thirty-eight she fell in love, for the first time — with a man who slept with the abandon of a child. He taught M. to relax. To stay in bed on a Saturday until midday. To have an orgasm. And for the first time in her life M. slept soundly by a man and discovered the sweetness of an arm winging her torso in slumber and the arch of a foot locked into her calf and waking with someone into the cleanness of a new day.

I can imagine a time when I may lose my taste for sex, but I know I'll never lose my desire for shared sleep. I leave you with D.H. Lawrence, again.

'It was cold, and he was coughing. A fine cold draught blew over the knoll. He thought of the woman. Now he would have given all he had or ever might have to hold her warm in his arms, both of them wrapped in one blanket, and sleep. All hopes of eternity and all gain from the past he would have given to have her there, to be wrapped warm with him in one blanket, and sleep, only sleep. It seemed the sleep with the woman in his arms was the only necessity.'

D.H. LAWRENCE — 'LADY CHATTERLY'S LOVER'

∞

*Surrender can require just as much strength
as resistance. It brings relief and freedom
and enlightenment. And often the higher ground,
with the grace of it.*

∞

Six

EXPRESSIONS FOR DOWN BELOW

Mistakes

that may be remedied…

'The language of sex had yet to be invented.'

ANAÏS NIN

Part I

INFERIORITY COMPLEXES

I've always felt that men who use the c-word don't like women very much.

Where are the expressions that women have colonised for themselves: the affectionate, positive, empowering ones?

L., a mother of two toddler daughters, says the situation is fraught, even in this day and age. That most of the words still in use are appalling or clinical or silly. That it still feels a little odd to say vagina in everyday conversation, and she's really not sure about pussy. Maybe we're ridiculously ignorant — but then so are a lot of our friends. We still use expressions like 'it' and 'nether regions' and 'down below', accompanied by an eye gesture downwards. Pathetic, I know, in this post-feminist world.

In the midst of this discussion a man called A. writes about what he perceives as a growing trend for men to treat women with scant regard, and for male frustrations at the world to manifest themselves in acts of violence and sexual misconduct. He cites the fact that girls now outperform boys at school, and women are making ever greater strides in the workplace. He foresees that male resentment towards women will only grow. Is it any coincidence that the c-word — so utterly demeaning to women — is becoming more accepted?

'No-one can make you feel
inferior without your consent.'

ELEANOR ROOSEVELT

Part II

LET US COLONISE THIS BRAVE NEW WORLD!

Let's make up some expressions. Affectionate, pleasurable, empowering ones. By women, for women.

> *Girls' best friend*
> *Hospitality suite*
> (I love these because they're fun, and
> they imply a cherishing.)

And then a cheeky enquiry becomes an avalanche of contributions:

> *Pleasuredome!*
> *Jade garden!*
> *Honeypot!*
> *BBT!* (Big Boy's Toy)
> A personal favourite? *Royal Enclosure.*
> 'Admittance to members only' is the helpful
> explanation.

Another favourite: *fanoir*. Its creator writes, 'I started using it years ago and it's caught on so much that people I don't even know now use it. It's doing the circuit. (Well, not mine personally, you understand.) Most women feel comfortable using it in company, including my daughter, who's eight.'

Mothers of daughters tell me they often come up with their own pet names: *Min*, *Belle*, *Precious Pearl*, *Twinkle*. The creator of the latter explains, 'It sounds vaguely mystical ('Twinkle Twinkle Little Star') and vastly superior to some of the alternatives. It's also something my husband can say at bath time — i.e., "Have you washed your twinkle?" without stammering like a teenage boy (men!).'

M.'s cautionary tale: 'Nikki, a word of warning. The expression for fig in Italian is alarmingly close to the one for female genitalia. I spent a whole year in Rome asking for a pound of pussy rather than fruit, which the boys in the market happily supplied — with huge smiles on their faces.'

'Boldness be my friend! Arm me, audacity...'

WILLIAM SHAKESPEARE

Seven

ADOLESCENT SEX

Much baffles our expectations...

'We, who sought many things, throw all away
for this one thing, one only.'

JUDITH WRIGHT — 'THE COMPANY OF LOVERS'

THE DRIFTING SPARK

How intriguing is that loss of spark and voice and certainty as some young girls travel through adolescence into womanhood.

Girls who were once so cheeky and unfettered and bold can seem lost as soon as a man puts his arm around them. Nabokov captured the firefly ephemerality of the journey in *Lolita* — his bolshy, shining young protagonist ends up drained in her late teens, pregnant and defeated by domesticity. She's waylaid her spirit and defiance, her stroppy ability to say 'No'. What's to blame?

I've watched S. grow up. I was in awe of her assurance at eleven — when I was debating marrying a boyfriend she said dryly, 'Wait and see what he's like when he's drunk.' Ah, such wisdom in one so young, I thought, she'll give men a run for their money. S. fell in love at sixteen, madly, overwhelmingly. She moved in with her lover. At nineteen they split and by then she'd lost her youth.

'I gave him everything,' she said later. 'I left school for him. Lost my esteem. Suddenly I couldn't stand up in a room and face people and I used to be so strong about everything. And, Nikki, he's weak, the weakest person I know.'

Why is there so often this leakage of confidence, the capitulation, as women become sexual? Virginity and chastity can seem like magic elixirs that make us calm, audacious, strong. I didn't find empowerment and mystery and grace in sex until well into my twenties.

Find your passion, something deep in your heart, a thing you love that isn't love. Pursue it with humour and perseverance and courage — the courage to listen to your deepest instincts and stick with them no matter what everyone around you is telling you to do. Don't give up. Be prepared to risk and fail and risk all over again, because if you keep on trying, you might one day succeed.

V., in her sixties, 'When they're younger, women see all the good in men and ignore the bad — but as they get older, they see all the bad and ignore the good.'

'Occupation is essential.'

VIRGINIA WOOLF

art II

FINDING GRACE

Those wilderness years of my youth, trying to find the sex of my imagination.

'If our sex life were determined by our first youthful experiments, most of the world would be doomed to celibacy,' is a quote popularly attributed to P. D. James. 'In no area of human experience are human beings more convinced that something better can be had if only they persevere.'

In some teen circles oral sex is seen as almost obligatory — a goodnight kiss. It's most often the girl who's providing it, as a way of maintaining a relationship. Many boys say it's about having fun while avoiding intimacy. It doesn't bode well for future relationships. Where's the respect? The cherishing of women?

Dr Helen Power, a lecturer on Women and Gender Studies at Washington University in St Louis, comments that oral sex is not a straightforward matter for young girls. 'If they're doing it to get boys and keep boys, and not doing it for their own sexual satisfaction, it seems quite sick. It's a sense of domination and a reaffirmation of the whole heterosexual idea that you'll do anything to have a boy or man in your life.'

I'm sorry but my body does not become flooded with pleasure while giving a blow job. In fact, it's often, inwardly, flinching from the task. (At the sheer *one-sidedness* of the process as much as anything, if it's performed in isolation; the audacity of such a selfish demand.) And if that kind of sexual experience is among a young woman's very first, well to me, that's a shame.

Is it impossible to request some *grace*? The only grace I remember in a teenage sexual experience was the first kiss. The tremulousness and scariness and utter loveliness of it.

'There is nothing like early promiscuous sex for dispelling life's bright mysterious expectations.'

IRIS MURDOCH

Part III

THE ALLURE OF THE FIRST

That first passion. Its vividness can whisper through our blood our entire lives, becoming the standard of intensity by which all other partnerships are measured.

E. writes, 'I've always felt there was a powerful bonding in that first relationship, a "joining" that's almost spiritual. Though I'm not a churchgoer, there's something about that first loving sexual relationship that's a spiritual "marriage". Rather than the soulless couplings to "get it out of the way", the friendship that grows into a sexual joining has a lasting mark on the heart.'

Limerence: a psychological term meaning an obsessive love, like a drug, a state of being addicted to the other person.

I think the key to the vividness of the first love is not holding back. We throw ourselves into it, often at an age when we're at our most insecure and vulnerable. We're raw, open, impetuous. We feel more alive than we've ever felt before. We don't love just a little, quietly or calmly; we're wild with love. As we get older a cautiousness closes over us.

'Desire, in my case, was an ardour
of the spirit...a savage ecstasy which
took possession of my brain.'

GEORGE SAND

Eight

THE DANGER OF FRENEMIES

Woman needs to
store energy, not expend it...

'*Friendships begin with liking or gratitude*
— roots that can be pulled up.'

GEORGE ELIOT

Part I

PIN-PRICKERS

Jessica Mitford called them frenemies. Those women in your life who you think are your friends, but then it dawns upon you that you never feel great about yourself when you're around them. They have an uncanny ability to reduce you, to nibble away at your buoyancy. What's the point of being around them?

An exercise: try saying to the flattener, next time you see them, 'You know what? Whenever I'm with you I never feel very good about myself. So I think we need a little distance.'

My unnamed frenemy, so vinegary. Holding back when she's kissed in greeting. Constantly niggling with reductive little barbs about work, appearance, children. Never quick to compliment.

The accumulation of pricks until your heart begins to flinch at the mere thought of the deliverer.

My frenemy is a master-pricker. And of course, she never sends thankyou notes or Christmas cards. I console myself with the fact her child never smiles.

Uh, that was savage. I felt this book suck in its breath at the writing of it.

Never sink to her level. Respond to cruelty with kindness. Experience how miraculously it can work.

Soften your belly, soften; forgive, move on. It's their problem, not yours. Have compassion for them. They're not worth expending energy upon and if you do, their presence will become larger and larger in your life. You can be sure that if you feel this way about them, others do too. Console yourself with that and have pity for them. Concentrate your energy upon the people who create good for you, the heart-lifters in your life.

'If it is abuse — why one is always sure to hear of it from one damned good-natured friend or another!'

RICHARD BRINSLEY SHERIDAN

Good manners and politeness come from love and happiness; generosity of spirit blooms from it. The occasions when we're ugly-spirited are the ones when we're feeling depleted and angry and hostile. Remember that, when people are horrible. They're probably going through a bad time themselves.

What goes around comes around.

Empathy. Do not underestimate the importance of that beautiful word, because empathy encourages kindness and kindness encourages a better world.

My grandfather said once, 'Never suppress a kind thought, honey.' He was right. It helps the giver as much as the receiver.

Every day H. does small, anonymous acts of goodness: dropping loose coins into a parking meter, letting drivers into her lane with a nod and a smile, tidying up her table at her café to help the waitress. She glows with this accumulation of small kindnesses, she walks through life as if she's perpetually chuffed. You can see it in her: it gives her a strength to endure, with grace.

'Keep away from people who try to belittle your ambitions. Small people always do that, but the really great make you feel that you, too, can become great.'

MARK TWAIN

FRENEMIES AT WORK

X. was a boss who was jealous of other women's achievements. She was only comfortable with people who were broken or hurting in some way. Happy, successful, contented people were a threat. She wanted to chip away at their equilibrium and make them as unhappy as she was, so she could then relate to them. I saw it again and again, and then I realised she was doing it to me, too.

It infected her face. The sourness of it in repose, when the mask had slipped.

Can't we women just be more supportive of each other? Life is hard. For all of us.

If you can't speak well of someone, don't speak of them at all. Attempt to be one of those people who never says a bad word about anyone. Well, I'm trying.

D.'s gift, the invisible cloak she suggests putting on in times of attack or fear. She says it goes down to your ankles and has a hood for your face if you need it. It protects you; it stops people from getting in and hurting you. You have to give it a colour; white perhaps.

To be truly free you have to forget what other people think of you.

My grandfather declared that the secret of his longevity was his placidness. 'I don't worry about things, honey,' he said at ninety-six. 'It's what keeps me going.'

Life is too short to be bound by other people's impressions of you, because then your world becomes a prison. And you can't control it.

∞

Love and success are great beautifiers.
But so is goodness.

∞

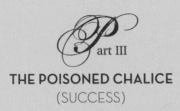

art III

THE POISONED CHALICE
(SUCCESS)

Often it's not when times are bad that you find out who your real friends are, but when times are good.

When I had a book success so many people disappeared from my life. It was such a distilling, clarifying time. But the true-blue ones, the handful I know I will have for life, were there. The rest, chaff.

Mum says if you have one true friend in life, you can forgive all the rest.

'Anybody can sympathise with the sufferings of a friend, but it requires a very fine nature to sympathise with a friend's success.'

OSCAR WILDE

Ah yes, those people who are quick to cluck and coo when word of a downfall comes; but will respond with vast, bewildering silence when there's joyful news. They're not there when you're experiencing the glow of great personal or work or financial success. It's as if they can't bear to have their emotions pricked by too much knowledge, or envy; it's too hard for them. They're not the kind of people who are going to lift your heart.

A supposed friend told me I was 'driven' and made it sound like a dirty word. I realised from that moment what I'd long suspected: she was uncomfortably competitive and a threat to my equilibrium. The distancing began.

'I was angry with my friend;
I told my wrath, my wrath did end.
I was angry with my foe:
I told it not, my wrath did grow.'

WILLIAM BLAKE

'I was taught that the way of progress
is neither swift nor easy.'

MARIE CURIE

Nine

TRANSCENDENCE

The power
of nature stirring our soul…

'Friday I tasted life. It was a vast morsel.
A Circus passed the house — still I feel the red in my
mouth though the drums are out. The lawn is full
of south and the odours tangle, and I hear to-day
for the first time the river in the tree.'

EMILY DICKINSON

Part I

THE PARTNER OF OUR DREAMS

C. is hugely annoyed by the female physiology. 'All our nerve endings are on the outside and not the inside — where they should be. We're built completely wrong.' She, like me, has never had a vaginal orgasm. She, like me, is in awe of the clitoris. And what it can transform women into.

Sex that includes an orgasm is the only time where we completely let go, when we show our partners our true selves. It jolts us into life, combusts us with light.

L. had me uttering sounds I have never uttered before, from the base of my spine. He was the first man I'd slept with who I actually fantasised about. It had taken a long time to find him.

He knew precisely what to do, and where. So many didn't.

Part II

THE GATEWAY

The clitoris is the only organ in the human body devoted purely to sensation. The little pleasure dome has eight thousand nerve endings. I repeat, eight thousand. Twice as many as the penis.

In Greek mythology, when Zeus and Hera visited the hermaphrodite, Tiresias, to determine whether it was men or women who experienced more pleasure from sex, Tiresias replied, 'If the sum of love's pleasure adds up to ten, nine parts go to women, only one to men.'

Surely even the tightest, most shut-down woman could be unlocked by oral sex — if it's done correctly. And if she allows it. 'He moved his lips about her ears and neck as though in thirsting search of an erogenous zone,' Joseph Heller wrote. 'A waste of time, he knew from experience. Erogenous zones were either everywhere or nowhere.' Well, not quite nowhere.

Problems: that partners can be too rough or too impatient or off target, or they've altered the rhythm at the crucial moment. Persistence, gentlemen, and patience. It takes women time to catch hold of an orgasm. And please, we don't want to feel like a lift button is being pressed, or an attempt is being made to rub a part of our body out.

That tip from somewhere: if it's just not happening for you, get your partner to pop an ice cube in their mouth.

Sex therapists often say that the number one complaint they hear from women is that they can't orgasm during vaginal intercourse. Clitoral stimulation, for a lot of us, is the only way we can come, consistently. Why aren't men taught that?

*'Sex seemed to me all surrender
— not the woman's to the man's
but the person's to the body.'*

ALICE MUNRO

art III

THE POWER OF POSITIVE THINKING

For P., it's all in the mind: 'The key for me is sexy sex. Experimenting with someone who's "dirt". You know, a guy who looks dirt — like they'd be into dirty, witty, cheeky sex.' She's thinking Johnny Depp at the moment.

'How many splendid loves I have dreamt of,' Rimbaud lamented. For some, the best sex they've ever had is the sex they've never had. We can be so much better at it by ourselves, in our imagination.

Stumbling across an old photo. The memory of his lips vivid under my fingertips.

Part IV

FOCUS, GENTLEMEN, FOCUS

'Sex pleasure in woman is a kind of
magic spell; it demands complete
abandon; if words or movements oppose
the magic of caresses, the spell is broken.'

SIMONE DE BEAUVOIR

Marlene Dietrich had a lover who smoked during sex. Well, she would, wouldn't she? I'm trying to imagine this as a sensual experience but can't quite get there. I'm sorry, but for a woman to enjoy mind-blowing sexual pleasure, she needs absolute focus. None of us like our men doing something else; we need to be flattered by full attention.

S. slept with a guy who kept on checking his watch. 'I was so insulted. I made up my mind there and then that I wouldn't be seeing him again. The weird thing is, I softened over the months. Was he timing himself? Trying to beat his own personal record?'

J. had a boyfriend who insisted on reading *Story of O* to her while he was stimulating her. 'But it was really off-putting because I wasn't sure exactly which activity I should be concentrating on.'

T.'s lover watched a football match on TV during sex. 'He kept on yelling "Score! Score!" His team didn't, and he didn't. T. walked out.

Distraction will kill the moment as swiftly as a power cut in a night-club. A woman who wants an orgasm out of sex needs to concentrate because they can be so darned elusive; so difficult to nudge out, so easily scared off if everything isn't quite right.

It's not unusual to be thinking of another scenario entirely as we're being made love to, one that has nothing to do with the person having sex with us. The mind is such a powerful tool when it comes to women and orgasms. And, of course, we don't always need a partner to kick-start the process.

Part V

IF THE SPIRIT MOVES US

'(Sex) was never dirty to me. After all, God gave
us the equipment and the opportunity. There's that
old saying, "If God had meant us to to fly, he'd have
given us wings." Well, look what he did give us.'

DOLLY PARTON

The ridiculousness of Christianity's insistence on separating
sex from spirituality.

Sexual intercourse is a deeply human experience and a
deeply mysterious one. Good sex is a spiritual experience
and the best sex is profound. At the height of sexual
ecstasy you're taken to another place and that place, above
all, is spiritual. Perhaps it's God's gift to us; his lure, his
little chuckle.

From sex comes that most magnificent decision in all of life
— to create it.

'Of all the delights of this world man cares most for sexual intercourse, yet he has left it out of his heaven.'

MARK TWAIN

Perhaps women are one step closer to eternity with our ability to carry a child. And I don't think it's at all surprising that a lot of girlfriends are refinding religion as they become mothers. Giving birth can be a profoundly spiritual process; the pinnacle of joy as a human being; a time when you're thanking God a lot.

Note to self: try reconsidering sex as a gift from God. Flood it with spirituality. For spirituality and sexuality are at the core of life. They shouldn't be separated or, good grief, denied.

'Contempt for sexuality is a crime against life.'

FRIEDRICH NIETZSCHE

Part VI

CANDLE GLOW

A different kind of transcendence — from an enduring partnership. Those exquisite little tremors, deep in your bowels, at the sight of a beloved partner after a long absence. Those soft little jolts unfurling through your groin at a voice on the phone in a country far away. These can be the sweetest shudderings of all, for the promise in them.

To aspire to: requited love.

An enduring relationship can be a partnership where the sex is infinitely more satisfying than snatched nights here and there, because with someone you know well it's possible to be so much more relaxed and experimental — and the sex, like fine wine, can improve over the years.

When I think of A. I think of that beautiful line from the Psalms, 'The darkness is no darkness with thee.' My love for him does not glitter, it glows strong and quiet like a candle. He is all-calming

Ten

WHAT WOMEN DON'T WANT

Objections that may
be raised…

'Friendship is the finest balm for
the pangs of despised love.'

JANE AUSTEN

Part I

AH, REMIND ME WHY I DID THIS?

E., who was sloppy with his love. It was a life of easy paths. He'd never change.

The man who resented what L. had. Not only in terms of more money, a better job and a nicer flat — but her vivacity, her spark. His challenge was to nibble away at that. And so we witnessed the tragedy of a strong, independent woman chipped away by her man. A not so unusual tragedy.

L.'s confidence was bled from her until she couldn't even go to work any more. He held her life hostage. When she said she couldn't work any more, because of him, I don't know who I was more angry with.

She spent all of her waking hours waiting for his call, his visit. Her life was suspended like a breath held. She could not see the damage he was doing — kidnapping her confidence and her strength.

The tragedy of a life bound by fear. The sinking heart when I heard, 'I feel that fear has dictated all my choices in life.'

To be undermarried as opposed to overmarried. What is worse? Assaulted by the piracy of indifference, or swamped by attention.

∞

It's so much healthier to want someone than to need them.

∞

Part II

NOT PROUD

Those one-night stands that were almost unbearably bleak. Where I'd end up thinking, 'Why did I do that?' and wondered if my sexual partner felt the same gulf of loneliness that I had.

So, ah, why *did* I do it? For that same reason that women do it again and again, despite living through all the empowerment of our post-feminist world. Because of the possibility of a thread, however tenuous, to the child, security, the nest. The possibility of a glowing New Year's Eve and a partner at Christmas lunch. I'm not proud to say it, but it's true.

We are animals. We are programmed to reproduce. We cannot deny our biological makeup.

E.'s love is like black-market money. Vast riches, but there's nowhere legitimate to deposit it.

The man everyone loved except his family. The warning in that.

R. didn't know how to relax. The relationship was exhausting, like being deprived of sleep.

He prized solitude above anything. He never enfolded any of his girlfriends with the calm of ownership, never gave any of them the gift of security. So while we were with him, we were obsessed. We were always thinking, 'When's this going to end?'

The pattern of easily breaking up, never committing, shouts of the person who never cares deeply enough.

I went back, again and again. Just as I was extricating myself he'd call and sleep with me and the spiral of exhilaration and terror would begin all over again. He was the rock upon which I would break and break. I wasn't meeting anyone else, of course.

Simone Weil said that the only real question to be asked of another person is: 'What are you going through?'

Part III

THE FATAL RETURN
(GRAVEYARD SEX – SEX WITH AN EX)

The shock of familiarity in our lovemaking. That matey tenderness of two people who knew each other extremely well. But as we lay in bed afterwards there was a blanket of memory over us, muffling any joy. We were careful not to touch in farewell, careful not to give each other anything to hold on to. We both knew that this melancholy, squalid, ghost-burdened little afternoon would never happen again. It was time, for both of us, to be free.

'Throw it away, it'll only give you worms in the head,' said my father, as he handed me the unopened letter from my ex-lover. Dad was right.

Take control of your life. Seize it.

Eleven

LEAPING

The old method of silence — a fatal mistake...

'Life is either a daring adventure or nothing.'

HELEN KELLER

Part I

BITING THE BULLET

Valentine's Day is all about the gift of attention. There's love, and indifference; the two cannot coexist. February 14 is that day of glorious opportunity when we can make up for those times, those many times, when we've lapsed, or been too afraid, or fortressed.

The haunting of lost opportunities. Why are we so cautious? So afraid of rejection and humiliation and exposure? We're often so embarrassed by those big declarations in life.

Just do it. So what if you fail? It makes us more approachable to our fellow human beings for it makes us less intimidating. Believe me, everyone else has known failure too.

Kindness is about lowering ourselves, as is being interested in someone, asking questions, giving them attention. 'Vivacity is surrender,' said the poet Les Murray — and why should that seem so demeaning?

S. is thirty-three. Several years ago, during Christmas dinner, his grandmother embarked upon the usual teasing-but-excruciating grilling about settling down. 'It's hard,' he replied, 'it's really hard.' The table hushed, shocked into silence by the honesty in his words. And then his aunt, who knew something of his past, said quietly, 'I don't think there's anyone in the world who doesn't want to be told they're loved.' And so in a Valentine's act of reckless kindness S. sent a note to the woman he'd been thinking about, every day, for the past five years. He lowered himself, he risked. For years he'd shied away from too much intimacy, fearing its ability to diminish him, to make him vulnerable. For years he'd been protecting himself — reacting instead of acting. But he suddenly realised that he had nothing to lose, and a lot to gain.

The two are now married.

She, too, had been kicking herself for years over failing to act.

Never underestimate the magnificence in embracing the unknown, surrendering to it.

*'Women should take more risks to live their
dreams, which otherwise turn into nightmares
of frustration as empty years pass.'*

EDIE LEDERER

Advice from an extremely glamorous great-aunt: 'Whenever a strange room is entered you must always remember four things, and repeat them silently to yourself as you cross the threshold: I am beautiful. I am witty. I am intelligent. And I can do whatever I want!'

And if leaping doesn't have the desired outcome, well at least you've tried and you have the solace of knowing that. As Katherine Mansfield said, 'When we begin to take our failures non-seriously, it means we are ceasing to be afraid of them. It is of immense importance to learn to laugh at ourselves.'

∞

Laughter keeps life — and risk — pleasurable.

∞

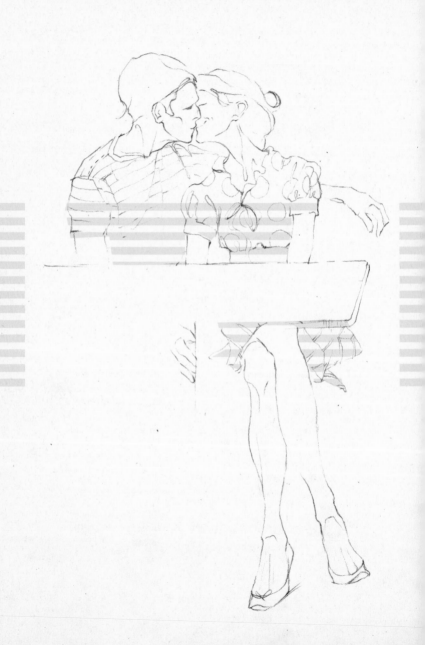

Twelve

THE KISS

he art of love...

'But indeed, dear, these kisses on paper are scarce worth keeping. You gave me one on my neck that night you were in such good–humour, and one on my lips on some forgotten occasion, that I would not part with for a hundred thousand paper ones.'

JANE CARLYLE — IN A LETTER TO THOMAS CARLYLE, 1826

WEARING AWAY OUR LIPS

A sexual kiss can be so much more personal than actual sex. And you have to be completely present for it — in the moment — whereas you don't have to be with intercourse.

Pablo Neruda wrote, 'wearing away our lips/from kissing each other's souls,' and you'd never get something as beautiful as that written about a blow job.

L., the man I'd been attracted to for half a decade. We'd never done anything about our mutual lust; for years we'd both stood back shyly, overwhelmed by caution, silently dreaming through various relationships the other person was having. We never declared an attraction to each other but both of us were achingly aware because of blushes and stumbly talk and stares a fraction too long.

Finally we were in the clear — both single. We kissed. It was completely, utterly wrong. We couldn't communicate on that most intimate of levels. It was like he'd read an instruction manual on how to kiss, how to move the tongue, the lips, but he'd never just...felt it.

I suspected that the lack of intimacy in L.'s kiss was a sign of things to come, and sure enough, when we made love there was a startling absence of tenderness as he jackhammered above me. I knew from that moment it wouldn't ever work. It had all been encapsulated in a kiss. The past six years of yearning vanished in a flash. I never saw him again.

Part II

THE THERAPEUTIC BENEFITS OF THE KISS

That passionate kiss that can arrest a relationship's slow, glacial slide towards indifference. One that can remind two people of how they used to be in love.

The tonic of it: 'I remember, yes, you're the man I fell in love with.'

In a relationship that was atrophying we tried kissing again like we had long ago, as first lovers. Remembering Robert Browning, the little pull in the belly I always got to at his tugging lines:

> 'The moth's kiss, first!
> Kiss me as if you made believe
> You were not sure, this eve.'

It worked.

Thirteen

BEREAVEMENT

Certain reflections…

'The dead don't die.
They look on and help.'

D.H. LAWRENCE

Part I

EMBRACE THE MYSTERY

In moments of grief, despair, crisis, we achieve lucidity. About who we are. And where we should go from here.

Death brings us closer to life.

Grief makes us so much more tender to other people's suffering. Enriches us as human beings in this complex, difficult, glorious world.

That beautiful line in the film *The Barbarian Invasions*, as the father lies dying, 'Embrace the mystery.'

The Scots believe you give up a life for a life.

The shock of hearing M.'s voice again, in a recording. The freshness of it plunges me back. Voice is so evocative, and how lucky if you have a recording of someone beloved.

A single command for my funeral — no flowers, no tears, but a simple wish. That everyone who cares enough goes and buys a gardenia plant for their garden or windowsill. Just that.

The tranquility of a death can be a reflection upon the vividness of a life lived. Those who are fulfilled — who have lived rich and compassionate and good lives — often pass peacefully. They are content. Grateful for the wonder in the journey.

Sister Maureen Flood, as she was nearing death said, 'My life is coming to end...I walk in darkness yet the darkness is luminous.'

Don't stop writing them letters. John Donne said, 'Letters mingle souls.'

Hearing on the radio, God gave us the gift of suffering.

*'What made us dream that
he could comb grey hair?'*

WILLIAM BUTLER YEATS

Part II

HEALING

Rabbis often end a memorial service with, 'May his memory be for a blessing,' i.e., what is the meaning of the dead person's life for those who are left behind? What lesson can they learn from the life that has passed?

Martin: to live your life passionately. To do what you really want to do.

Nora: the gift of friendship, the grace in her living, the importance of laughter.

Frank: it was all in his face. Joy. The shine of it near the end. As if his last years were spent in a perpetual state of chuckle at the wonder of it all.

Send a candle to someone who is remembering the anniversary of a death and is still grieving. There's something so comforting about the ritual of lighting a candle in memory of someone who has left us. We like to know others remember, too.

Light a candle for your beloved whenever the grief threatens to swamp you; to calm you, to bring you closer, to extend a hand and a soul.

Tim Lott recalls in his memoir, *The Scent of Dried Roses*:

> So it is on the anniversary of Jean's death that my father sits at home with no-one to share the grief with him…Yet there is a knock at the door and a distant neighbour to whom Jack has hardly ever spoken appears. She hands him a bottle of wine and says, 'I thought you might need this, tonight.' She asks how he is, smiles sweetly, and walks out into the night. For she has made a note of this date and cared enough about a stranger to remember through a whole year, and it reminds Jack of what he has always, in his heart, believed, which is that people, though often stupid and often blind, in the end wish to be good.

∞

Pain is like that tree being pruned to make it grow strong. And beautiful.

∞

Fourteen

CAPITULATION

trophy of instincts...

'How I regret now that perpetual emotional dependence on the man I love has killed all my other talents — my energy too: and I had such a lot of that once.'

SOFIA TOLSTOY

Part I

DINNER TIME!

America's former Secretary of State, Madeleine Albright, was once one of the world's most powerful women. This is what she said about being a wife: 'In the twenty-three years I was married to Joe, his tastes became mine. After he left, I rediscovered the fact that I didn't like beef — even though for years we had eaten it almost every night.'

Ah, so even Madame Secretary — entrusted with the foreign policy of one of the world's strongest nations — has known, in her private life, the creep of capitulation; how much a woman's most basic choices can be reoriented by her partner.

A food nutritionist, Ian Marber, says of his freshly divorced patients: 'They've usually been comfort-eating their way through life, and have adopted the eating habits of the dominant partner.' Don't we all know the newly single woman who drops several dress sizes — because she can suddenly skip the evening meal. Or just have toast.

When my husband's away I…uncurl.

'Your life is how the other person would like it to be,' Jerry Hall said of her marriage to Mick Jagger. And if many women can capitulate over such basic things as what they eat, what of sex?

What woman has sex exactly the way she wants to, as opposed to the way her partner wants it?

Show me the woman who's never done something sexually that she would have preferred not to. Does that warrior woman exist? Would any man dare go near her?

That mouldering bitterness in some of those women who've come of age in the 1940s and 1950s. Throughout their lives have they acted as they wished to, have they owned their lives? Their anger has festered over the years at the sabotaging of the promise that was in them when they were young. Promise leached away by circumstance, by marriage and motherhood. They have taken out their despair on their daughters and their husbands and then in old age they've looked back with anger and regret. The tragedy of it.

'There are many ways of breaking a heart.
Stories were full of hearts broken by love, but what
really broke a heart was taking away its dream —
whatever that dream might be.'

PEARL S. BUCK

We want love too much, and for many of us, children. We want to please, maintain a relationship, it's in our blood. So we capitulate.

I wish I knew the solution. Katherine Mansfield thought she had it in 1908. 'Here is a little summary of what I need: power, wealth and freedom. It is the hopelessly insipid doctrine that love is the only thing in the world, taught, hammered into women, from generation to generation, which has hampered us so cruelly.'

We haven't freed ourselves from the pursuit of love, despite all the feminist advances of recent decades. We never will. I wonder, now, what Miss Mansfield would be more astounded by — a woman in charge of the foreign policy of the world's most powerful nation or the fact that that woman had eaten something she didn't like almost every night of her married life.

'I could easily have been a Daisy Flett.
One of those women who erases herself,
who somehow slips out of her own life.'

CAROL SHIELDS

Part II

THE DIGNITY IN RISK

'All the strength you need to achieve anything is within you. Don't wait for a light to appear at the end of the tunnel, stride down there...and light the bloody thing yourself.'

SARA HENDERSON

The aim: to manage your life rather than simply let it happen to you. So much unhappiness stems from a lack of control.

The most important lesson my mother taught me was to never rely on a man for my quality of life, to always be financially independent. Because with independence comes strength.

Driving gives women a great sense of strength and independence. It's no surprise that so many Muslim women are forbidden to drive. There's a subversive freedom to it, the thrill of independence.

'One is happy as a result of one's own efforts,
once one knows the necessary ingredients of happiness
— simple tastes, a certain degree of courage,
self-denial to a point, love of work, and above all,
a clear conscience. Happiness is no vague dream,
of that I now feel certain.'

GEORGE SAND

∞

You shape your life, no-one else. That is what it means to be a woman today.

∞

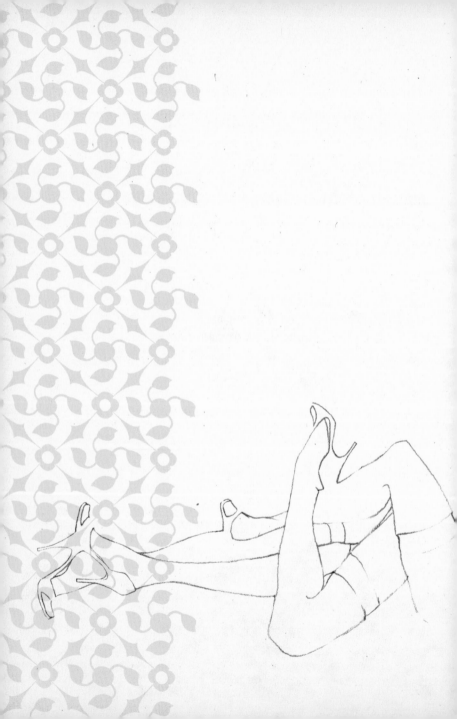

Fifteen
LESBIANISM

tremendous adventure...

*'Next to my own skin, her pearls. My mistress
bids me wear them, warm them, until evening
when I'll brush her hair. At six, I place them
round her cool, white throat. All day I think of her...'*

CAROL ANN DUFFY — 'WARMING HER PEARLS'

THE CAT WITH THE RICHEST CREAM

'Darling, we have fingers, tongues and plastic,' C. says, 'and it's amazing what we can do with them.' She's experienced both men and women and has come down firmly on the side of her own gender.

'I truly believe you can have a deeper sexual experience with someone of your own sex. Because if you know exactly what the other person's feeling — if you can read their mind — then the experience can be mind-blowing. And, darling, let's be honest, women know what women want.' A pause. 'And where…' She smiles, the cat with the richest cream.

N. is celebrating the new, cool bi-curiosity: 'There are so many issues we have to deal with — like homophobic parents for a start. And if all those people who are giving us a hard time are seeing in the newspapers that these women are empowered and successful and normal — then hallelujah, that's a giant leap for everyone.'

C. says the whole point is being honest with yourself. And that the majority of people need to make up their mind.

She says gay people are often more honest with themselves — and honesty, naturally, results in better sex.

'Ok,' bluntly, 'so why exactly do you prefer women?'

'It's the most exquisite lovemaking imaginable,' N. replies softly. 'And for a lot of us, there's an element of trust in there. You know you're not going to be abused or physically overpowered. And you can usually say no to something you don't like. How often does that normally happen?'

Indeed.

Part II

THE COURAGE OF OUR CONVICTIONS

To be openly gay requires an enormous amount of courage. The courage to live honestly. To declare to the world who you really are.

A magazine survey found that sixty-five per cent of women admit to fantasising about other women. And among these openly bi-curious younger chicks there's no talk of a secretive, oppressed minority.

'I love these new feminine free spirits,' N. declares. 'They're so much more confident than my own generation. They've got the freedom to be honest with themselves. What a wonderful climate to be able to say these things openly — and not be judged!'

The one thing she's not sure about are young women who may be dipping into bisexuality because it's cool — or worse, as a means to impress a boyfriend. The columnist Taki wrote, 'Like most men, I am consumed with desire whenever a lesbian gets within twenty feet.' That old male fantasy, two for the price of one.

N. hopes these young women are liberating a deep-seated urge, rather than merely dabbling in a fashionable lifestyle choice. She says no sexual relationship should be treated as a fling — straight or gay — because if that's the case, it's denigrating for everyone involved. 'I've no time whatsoever for the female equivalent of a cock-teaser. A clit-teaser! Aaaah!'

'The public does not matter
— only one's friends matter.'

WILLIAM BUTLER YEATS

Secrets sap us and stunt our growth; they can become huge, dominate our lives. When we hold something in, it becomes a great burden, difficult to shed. Grasp the relief in exposure. The dignity in risk. You might be surprised at the outcome, for it's amazing how much support you get when you tell the truth.

Sixteen

HOW TO IMPROVE OUR LOVE LIVES

An attempt
to find the remedy…

'The great question that has never been answered and which I have not yet been able to answer despite my thirty years of research into the feminine soul, is "What does a woman want?"'

SIGMUND FREUD

Part I

EXUBERANCE IS BEAUTY

Marilyn Monroe said, 'I don't think I do it properly.' What a relief to read it.

No-one is born a lover, it has to be learnt.

I used to believe expertise came with age until, in my early twenties, I slept with P. He was almost thirty years older than me. He was from an era when sex was purely for the man's satisfaction. He had pre-AIDS notions of birth control (it was the woman's duty to go on the pill, no matter how much it may affect her physically; condoms were a joke). He also had very strong thoughts about older women. He'd never sleep with anyone over thirty; he didn't like them enough — the sagging skin on their necks, the lines on their faces, their bodies thickening out. But I know another reason now — it's because women beyond thirty have lost their docility. They know too much.

And want things themselves.

W. confesses over scones and tea that she loves sex on top — a sure sign of body confidence. A lot of women don't like it because it feels like they're on display. W. declares it's empowering, and as I listen and watch her I think, sexy has nothing to do with cleavage — it's all about confidence.

M. gives the impression of a woman who loves laughing in bed. She's a healthy size fourteen and she's comfortable with that. Men love a woman who loves her body. 'Exuberance is beauty,' said William Blake.

C. is twenty-seven. She's an archivist, a collector of sexual experiences — she recently had a party to celebrate her fiftieth sexual partner ('There'll be another for my hundredth!'). She's worked out that the best way to orgasm while a man's inside her is to angle him so he's rubbing against her pelvic bone and stimulating her clitoris. She makes love audaciously, positioning her men exactly where she wants them.

She loves being single because, she says, you're determined to get an orgasm out of every sexual experience. 'Unlike people in long-term relationships, where it doesn't matter so much.' 'Why?' 'Because they've got a lot more time to experiment and relax. To risk not having an orgasm.'

The thought of having sex heroically; of doing exactly what you've always wanted to.

A.'s delight at cracking me open. Discovering my sexual voice.

What I've learnt: that periods of low desire in a long-term relationship don't necessarily spell doomsday; the embers of romance can be stoked into flame again. It requires a willingness to do battle with complacency and invisibility. My tactic at the moment is surprise.

The tenderness of the unexpected.

Part II

THE SECRET OF WATER

F. writes: 'Nik, the easiest and most guaranteed way of attaining heavenly bliss is in the shower, with a hand-held power-shower. I find water very erotic; the soft yet forceful jets stimulate the right place without even having to lay a finger on it! It brings a whole new meaning to going to the gym. After exercise I often have a flutter in the shower — it's even more erotic being in a public place where you might get caught. It also works well with a partner (not advised in the gym though!) as even the most uncertain fumblers can direct a shower head vaguely in the right direction.'

C. has recognised a swimming pool's potential for years: 'I've had magnificent water orgasms. It started when I was a teenager, in our family pool. I'd swim to the edge and find a filter hole the size of a fifty cent coin with water coming out at high pressure. I'd hang my feet up on the edge of the pool and that magic feeling would come within minutes.'

Part III

DARKER PATHS

A sexually confident forty-eight year old tells me that lovemaking with her husband was becoming infinitely more pleasurable as the years have passed. 'And darker,' the mother of four smiles contentedly. 'I'm a lot more relaxed now that all the worries about making babies — or not making them — have passed.' Then she adds, bewildered, 'Why should experimental sex be associated, for so many women, with pain and fear, when that is the way pleasure lies?'

Why indeed — as long as they're going down that path of their own free will. Those legendary twelfth-century lovers, Abelard and Heloise, were gleeful exponents of sex beyond convention. 'Our desires left no stage of lovemaking untried, and if love could devise something new, we welcomed it,' Abelard wrote. 'We entered on each joy the more eagerly because of our previous inexperience and were all the less easily sated.' I think the key word there is joy. Those two deeply religious, searingly intelligent people were having a huge amount of fun. As is my forty-eight year old.

A joyous letter from a woman unlocked:

Dear Nikki,

I'd not had sex with my husband for ten years; he never had much of a sex drive. Then after divorcing at fifty-five I had sex with another man (found through the website Friends Reunited. He's my age, from my old infant school, even though we don't remember each other from then.) The sex was fantastic! So last year I signed up to an online dating service and I've probably had more sex recently than in my entire marriage. Never let it be said all women hate sex. I have a very high libido which had been wasted for over thirty years. I'm a different person now — it's done wonders for my self-esteem.

∞

𝒮urround yourself with people who are the heart-lifters not the heart-sinkers.

∞

Part IV

NOTES ON A TECHNICAL UNPLEASANTRY

Well, I certainly can't speak for all women, but to me fellatio is about as appealing as cleaning the oven or defrosting the fridge. It's not just the unpleasantness of it — there's a humiliation factor. I don't feel empowered as a woman when I'm doing it, I don't feel I'm having sex in the way I'd like to. There's also something so bleak and lonely about it. From the woman's perspective, there's a lack of intimacy. Anyone could be doing it.

'Oral sex is just for prostitutes,' declares Z., in her sixties. She's proud of the fact she's never done it. 'There's no dignity in it.'

Part V

SEX AND THE SENSES

There's something deeply erotic about making love without sight. Perhaps it's why so many women like sex with the lights off — and it's not simply to obscure the size of our thighs. There's the hope of heightened tenderness and closeness as we're forced to rely on other senses, and the lovely anticipation of surprise.

Going where we've never been is a deeply seductive concept, as is arriving at a familiar destination in a freshly inventive way. No wonder the silk blindfold is such a popular sex toy. The harsh glare that lights so much porn strips sex of mystery. Darkness bathes it in it.

Sex after a drought can be astonishing. All your senses are deliciously sensitive and receptive. Like the first, exquisite morsel of your favourite dish after a very long fast.

'I shut my eyes in order to see.'

PAUL GAUGIN

art VI

SEXY LINES

'I am in love with moistness.'

GEORGE ELIOT

'Might I but moor
Tonight in thee!'

EMILY DICKINSON

'You have bereft me of all words, lady.'

WILLIAM SHAKESPEARE

'She smells of the sea. She smells of rock pools when
I was a child. She keeps a starfish in there. I crouch
down to take the salt, to run my fingers around
the rim. She opens and shuts like a sea anemone.
She's refilled each day with fresh tides of longing.'

JEANETTE WINTERSON

Action — acting rather than reacting — cultivates exhilaration.

The clue we were seeking...

'Many will bite the usual bait:
They will talk their slippery way
through fine clothes and expensive perfume,
fishing up your independence.

These are,
The did-you-come-yets of the western world,
the feather and fin rufflers.
Pity for them they have no wisdom.

Others will bite at any bait.
Maggot, suspender, or dead worm.
Throw them to the sharks.

In time one will crawl
out from under thigh — land.
Although drowning he will say,

"Woman I am terrified, why is the house shaking?"

And you'll know he's the one.'

RITA ANN HIGGINS
— 'THE DID-YOU-COME-YETS OF THE WESTERN WORLD'

Part I

COULD YOU TURN UP THE VOLUME, PLEASE?

And so I turn to the gentlemen for this chapter. Specifically, one gentleman in particular who is used to conducting forums, and has a captive group — twelve men in a pub.

To the very first question, 'What do you like your wife to do while you're having sex?' initially come the kind of responses that, well, you'd expect from twelve men in a pub: 'Go shopping.' 'Cook dinner.'

But then the conversation settles, and the honesty, suddenly, comes thick and fast. 'The first dislike,' my intrepid researcher reports back, 'is bad oral sex.' Ah, yes? 'You know, teeth on the penis, which is painful and not nice. Second is a bad hand job — girls thrashing away with no lubricant. Are we supposed to like this?' He's on a roll now, despite protestations to slow down, stop, please.

'As for things we guys love, we all agreed we want a verbal response. Just a few oohs and aahs from you women are worth so much. Silence, Nikki, is not golden.' He explains that he still recalls, years later, a lover going, 'Oooh, that's great' as he hit the spot.

Part II

WHAT MEN DO NOT WANT

'Let's make a baby.'
'I feel like a whale, please can we turn off the light?'
'Already?'

A lack of enthusiasm. I have many, many letters on this topic:

> *Dear Nikki,*
>
> *I do not want to feel that my partner's just
> going through the motions. I can live with poor
> technique and the fact she isn't as slim as she
> once was — who is? But if you love someone, and
> yet get the feeling that during sex she's really not
> interested, it's such an enormous turn off.*

> *Dear Nikki,*
>
> *Women like to feel loved, desired, attractive.
> Well, Nikki, we feel exactly the same (only don't
> like to admit it, certainly not to other men). We
> want a woman to be as noisy as possible. Verbal*

*encouragement is the biggest turn on — because it
confirms desire on her part.*

Dear Nikki,

   *If the man's always the one to propose sex
eventually we feel like a small kid pestering Mum for
sweets — unwanted, undesirable and a nuisance.*

Dear Nikki,

   *Like you lot, we men are full of doubts,
insecurities and fears about our attractiveness
and desirability — but we'd rather die than admit
it. We know you're afraid your bum looks too big
but we really don't mind. So please, please, don't
turn the light off. We're not Brad Pitt, either —
but hope you'll be so turned on that you'll forget!*

And from a correspondent quite cross: 'Too many women
seem to believe that sex is a spectator sport. It'd be good if
they joined in occasionally.'

There are also, surprisingly, requests for guidance: 'You
know, Nikki, it's really hard for us guys when you women
lie on the bed with the intention of quantifying our sexual
ability from one to ten, with no prior verbal input, and then
expect us to give you total fulfilment.'

R. tells me he hates going down on a woman because it always makes him gag. He can't stand the taste, even though, he says, every woman is different. What lover has ever intimated anything like that to me? R. is an ex-colleague and I have absolutely no interest in him sexually, likewise him with me. How much easier it is to be completely honest when there's no sexual tension between you.

A final plea, from Mr Bewildered: 'It'd be nice if women would just say what they like, instead of us always having to guess. Oh, and if they could just be a little more adventurous.'

'The majority of husbands remind me of an orangutan trying to play the violin.'

HONORÉ DE BALZAC

∞

*Don't be afraid of sharing your vulnerabilities —
your fear, envy, frustration. It will make you
realise how alike we all are. You'll be amazed to
hear again and again, 'Yeah, me, too.'*

∞

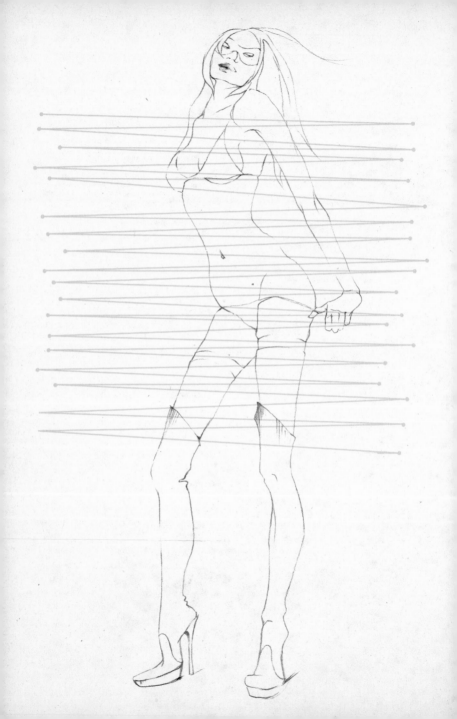

Misuse of the word love...

*'Pornography is rather like trying to find
out about a Beethoven symphony by having somebody
tell you about it and perhaps hum a few bars.'*

ROBERTSON DAVIES

Part I

BLEAK HOUSE

That seduction by the flatmate in my late teens who used the porn video 'to get me in the mood'. That memory of being fascinated, at first, and yes, turned on — but then quickly repelled. The sex we had afterwards was mechanical, bleak, ugly. There was an utter absence of tenderness or inventiveness. The flatmate left the room as soon as he'd climaxed. The next morning we barely spoke and never made reference again to that evening or that video. I moved out soon after.

Such a sour, squalid little night.

Seperated by a vast canyon of unconnecting and there is such a sadness to an experience like that; such an absence of soul or grace. Two desperately lonely people were connecting— but utterly failing to at the same time.

Porn strips sex of mystery — of reverence and transcendence. Several of my partners over the years have consumed porn to varying levels, and no matter how much they've proclaimed it's harmless, it's always made me uneasy. Why? Because I've felt it's sucked energy from the relationship, it's deadened the magic and messiness of interaction between two people. It steals away reliance upon a lover for sexual arousal.

Porn is sex with no light in it, and the best sex is bursting with light and life. You cannot be intimate without courage and there's nothing courageous about porn. It's sex and interaction made easy. The hard bit, of course, is real life, where people are much more insecure about relationships. And their own sexual performance.

> *'Life shrinks or expands in*
> *proportion to one's courage.'*

> **ANAÏS NIN**

Part II

RUSKIN'S PHOBIA

In the real world women aren't always available. In the real world they aren't always pandering to the male ego. In the real world most women don't look like those in a lot of erotica — shaved, with breasts like bowling balls.

Repetition kills the soul.

Porn is all about what men can do to women, rarely the other way around. It's about men exercising control over women — who are always available. Life is far messier than that.

What do young men, introduced to sex through porn, actually think when they're confronted by a regular woman's normality? Her physical imperfections, her emotional insecurities and needs? Ruskin idolised women so much he couldn't consummate his marriage when he discovered, to his horror, that his wife had pubic hair.

I wonder if some men drift further and further into porn because it's so much easier than the challenge of a real relationship.

art III

A SLIGHT DIVERSION INTO SEXUAL AMBIGUITY

The Mona Lisa. *What* is that woman's story? She's a mass of erotic contradictions. Sober clothes and demurely folded hands and yet, the smile.

It's a painting that has a huge amount to do with sex and it's a big reason, I suspect, why it's still so alluring five hundred years on.

'The idea that two distinct elements are combined in Mona Lisa's smile is one that has struck several critics. They accordingly find in the beautiful Florentine's expression the most perfect representation of the contrasts that dominate the erotic life of women; the contrast between reserve and seduction, and between the most devoted tenderness and a sensuality that is ruthlessly demanding.'

SIGMUND FREUD

Da Vinci gloriously captures a type of sexual contradiction, a particularly female one: hints of a private, supremely confident eroticism behind the sternest of public masks. And who is one of the most powerfully ambivalent women around today? The only one, besides a model or a prostitute, who's regularly paid more than a man?

The stripper.

And what a mass of erotic contradictions she is: a woman who promises everything but ultimately gives very little. It's all look and fantasise — but don't touch, let alone possess. She's a woman who's completely in control, never going all the way. And she revels in that supreme moment of power where she has the rapt attention of the room and is calling all the shots. What could be more intriguing, contrary and surprising than that?

So, my friend, in this chapter I leave you with the Mona Lisa and the stripper: two examples of womanhood that seem at opposite ends of the spectrum. But that combination of sex withheld, and a mysterious, confident eroticism is an extremely powerful one.

And it's worked in both instances, for centuries.

Nineteen

AFFAIRS

for others the temporary union...

'Let's face it, I have been momentary.
A luxury. A bright red sloop in the harbor.
My hair rising like smoke from the car window.
Littleneck clams out of season.
She is more than that. She is your have to have...'

ANNE SEXTON — 'FOR MY LOVER, RETURNING TO HIS WIFE'

art I

THE BIG QUESTION

Would you stay with your partner if they were having an affair? I've faced that dilemma. L.'s secretary invited me for coffee and informed me that her boss, my boyfriend, had a woman in every port, including the city we were all living in; and in this city the woman was herself. She said our mutual lover had spoken of all his current conquests with her. 'What did he say about me?' I stammered, in shock. 'It would be lies anyway,' she smiled sympathetically. Oh masterful game!

As I walked away from that cunning little secretary, my world turned upside down. I thought of the man I barely knew. There'd been no sense, ever, of love as a rescue. I'd always wanted a relationship like a hand in the small of my back as I walked up a hill — a partnership that was supportive, strengthening, nurturing — but it had always felt like I was in freefall; terrifying, exhilarating, exhausting. His secretary fought for him. I didn't. I suspected he'd repeatedly break the heart of any woman he ended up with; I wouldn't ever completely trust him.

I never went back.

> *'Courage is the price that life extracts
> for granting peace.'*

AMELIA EARHART

It's extremely hard to seduce someone who's content. An affair needs dissatisfaction, uncertainty, insecurity.

I imagine sleeping with almost every man I meet, weighing them up, yes or no. It's what you do about it that's the key.

Part II

WOMEN WHO STAY

Those upper middle-class English women who endured their husband's philandering: Jimmy Goldsmith's Annabel, Alan Clark's Jane. They made a difficult situation work with grace and stoicism. Crucially, they both described their husbands as loving when they were with them. Both cited their children as the reason they wanted the marriage to survive. But when Jimmy Goldsmith established his third concurrent family, Annabel consulted a lawyer. 'This was at the stage when, you know, it did hurt,' she explained. 'And he said, "Well, just ask yourself this question: do you want to stay married or not?" The answer was I preferred to stay married.'

Jane Clark has said that at times she detested her husband; but she, too, wanted the marriage. There was immense pain for both women but at the end of the day immense love.

Some couples who've weathered infidelity contract into an intriguing tightness in old age. The wives attain an inviolable position of power.

In one sense it's sensible, practical. But in another it's dispiriting. I'd prefer someone who embodies Courtney

Love's summation of Kurt Cobain: 'Sex, to him, was incredibly sacred. He found commitment to be an aphrodisiac.'

Call me foolish or romantic or just plain younger; but perhaps it's a new generation of women that demands a different way of being valued.

The French, of course, are famously more sophisticated in these matters, more accepting that men must have their affairs. Yet several French women I know have an immense sadness in their faces, as if they've endured a lifetime of being let down.

It's also the feminist in me that bristles at these scenarios. My question about equality to these husbands is: Would you be happy for your wives to also enjoy lovers? I don't think so.

Norman Lindsay said, 'The best love affairs are those we never had.'

Part III

RE-FINDING YOURSELF

B. says she trusts herself again, after finding out about E.'s affairs. 'About ten years ago I just felt I couldn't sleep with him. I didn't want to, didn't know why. And now I know that ten years ago was when the affairs began. Now I understand and trust what I felt. My body was right. It was telling me something.'

She's cracking open a whole new life. Doing things, finally, that she's always wanted to do. She looks young, girly, alive — freed.

Perhaps whether you stay and endure, or leave, depends on how much self-esteem you have. How much confidence as a woman.

Anger that's controlled is a wonderful impetus to achieving in life.

Twenty

THE IDEAL HUSBAND
A CHECKLIST TO CUT OUT AND KEEP

he great cause
of happiness in marriage…

'Poetry, like all passion, seeks for peace.'

RUTH PITTER

My DREAM MAN...

Treats his partner as a woman, not merely a wife ☐

Respects what she wants in bed and precisely where ☐

And what she doesn't ☐

Has a touch that's tender, slow, provocative ☐

Loves laughing in bed ☐

Never comes on his wife's breasts or face ☐

Never forces her to swallow his cum ☐

Never gives her underwear involving leopard print or red satin or gaps in crucial places, let alone expects her to wear it ☐

Never sustains the vaginal sex for so long it veers into pain; never thrusts so hard it hurts ☐

Doesn't expect his wife to be subservient to his pleasure at the expense of her own ☐

Never flattens her spirit; is a heart-lifter as opposed to a heart-sinker ☐

Never tries to reduce her or wear her down ☐

Is not intimidated by her achievements ☐

Understands that his wife may need a career to spine her life, and doesn't expect her to be confined to the home ☐

Tells her she's beautiful; reminds her to love her body ☐

Recognises the life-affirming qualities in kindness, the pleasure given in the simplest of gestures — a cup of tea, unasked; a favourite magazine picked up from the newsagent; unexpected flowers; the gift of a Saturday morning lie-in; a bath run ☐

Gives his wife the gift of attention ☐

Is not cynical about commitment, or her friends, or a woman's desire to sometimes be alone ☐

Cherishes his mother but doesn't expect his wife to be her ☐

Doesn't leave his loose change in little piles around the house ☐

Picks up wet towels and puts his dirty clothes in the clothes basket ☐

Is extremely comfortable with rolling down the car window and asking for directions ☐

Never asks, 'What are you thinking?' or 'How was it for you?' or 'Where's my dinner?' ☐

Lets his wife occasionally have the remote control ☐

Is comfortable with saying 'I love you', a lot ☐

Is a haven, a harbour, for rest from all the toss of the world ☐

Makes his wife laugh, even when she's down (especially when she's down) ☐

∽

Begin each day with three thank yous.
Gratitude leads to contentment, which leads to joy.
And joy is a most effective medicine.

∽

Twenty-one

MOTHERHOOD

The siren woman and the maternal woman...

'*...Your lips are animals; you are fed with love.*'

ANNE SEXTON — 'UNKNOWN GIRL IN THE MATERNITY WARD'

THE PRAM IN THE HALL

That guilty secret of my thirties — that I longed to throw in the career, after years of solid work, and be a housewife for a while. It felt mucky to admit it; my mother had always told me I must never rely on a man. But I did. There were two children in quick succession and it was a relief, to be honest, the surrendering of the feminist wariness. It felt naughty and delicious and indulgent, like wearing a bit of fur. (But then eventually I had to get back into the real world. Needed it.)

Conception: what I now had was a knowledge of the sacred. For I'd never had a more profound sexual experience than when my partner and I decided to conceive. All the mystery and power of the sexual act was brought into focus. This, deep down, was what this whole business was all about.

The woman at the party who talked of 'squeezing a last baby out of her husband'. Oh yes, pumping hard, squeezing tight, milking the sperm.

Pregnancy: as if all the nerve endings were tuned as finely as a concert grand's strings.

D.'s nerve endings were tuned a little too finely. When her baby was born her sexual high continued just as intensely, and she had to stop breast-feeding after a couple of weeks because every time her baby suckled she'd have an orgasm. She said it was delightful at first, then exhausting.

She's now on her fourth child because, she says, she never feels better than when she's pregnant. She revels in her happy hormones.

Her advice for labour: 'Just remember, "My vagina is a slippery dip." Chant it over and over in your head.'

The warning: 'Sex after birth is like throwing a sausage down the Sydney Harbour Tunnel.'

Part II

NOTES ON MISCARRIAGE

Cry, and cry again. It's a bereavement.

Some people may not be able to talk to you about it. That's their problem, not yours.

It's amazing, chatting to other women, how many of them have been through it also. And how wrenching it made them feel too.

Don't feel like a failure, that you've done something wrong or that you can't ever carry a baby successfully to term — a miscarriage is often, ultimately, a blessing. This little one wasn't meant to be, for a reason.

I know it's hard to imagine in the thick of it, but the body is often incredibly fertile after a miscarriage, more so than ever before. You can feel an almost-animal pull to do it all over again. The wonders of nature.

Part III

DOCTOR IN THE HOUSE

'I rushed to the loo before seeing my gynie,' J. giggles, 'and there was no loo paper, so I grabbed a tissue out of my handbag. The doctor was mystified to find a stamp stuck to my nether regions!'

Would you ever find a gay gynaecologist?

P. recalls, 'He gave me stitches without even asking me — he was so…invasive. And patronising. I much preferred the midwife.'

J. was appalled when the doctor started questioning her a little too thoroughly about how vigorously her sex life had been revived, post-baby. 'It was too…voyeuristic.'

'But maybe we're all becoming a little too jittery,' S. remarks. She says her private gynie would do anything to avoid examining her nether regions. 'Don't you want to see my bits?' she asked him desperately in the end. He never did.

Both K. and S. feel that in the private sector, it often amounts to business and marketing. 'Two private gynies informed me I was "treatably infertile",' explained K. 'Bling bling!' (She went on to conceive two children naturally.)

'I reckon it's all about power,' K. concludes. 'And having a good old look.'

I summon up the courage to ring the only male obstetrician I vaguely know, socially, and ask him why exactly he does what he does. 'Well...it just brings you closer to the whole source and mystery of life. I feel very privileged.'

Ah, lovely answer! It doesn't sate the curiosity though.

The smile at the doctor's line of questioning at the eight week check-up after birth. They're always so eager to hear you've been having lots of healthy, rollicking sex. Both times I've wanted to say, 'Honey, I was ripped in childbirth and endured the agony of stitches and constipation for quite a few weeks afterwards. And you know what? Sex is about the last thing on my mind.' Of course, I've never said this. I've just slunk home, wondering what's wrong with me.

'The animals put us women to shame — we've forgotten how to give birth joyfully. But I've never regretted the pain I went through: people say that children who are carried so high in the womb and take so long to come down towards the light are always deeply loved children, since they have chosen to lie right next to their mother's heart, and are reluctant to leave it...'

COLETTE

OUT AND ABOUT

Those stay-at-home mothers who have maternity nurses, then full-time nannies and weekend nannies when their regular nanny has time off. What are they afraid of? How can they really, deeply know their children?

Ask a nanny if she'd ever raise her own child in a similar way; the answer, invariably, is a telling no.

I love how babies smell of all the people who have held them. Their skin is so absorbent, a blueprint of attention.

The man at the party who travels regularly to the other end of the city to smell his newborn niece's head; he says it's the most powerful, non-erotic human experience. 'Go on, do it, just smell a baby's head,' he urges and I want to hug his enthusiasm. 'Especially the double cream,' he adds. 'That little dip at the back of their necks, at the nape. It's so soft.'

Hurrying past the elderly woman on the way to my son's school. 'I bet that's a boy,' she announces without turning, as I'm about to overtake her on the footpath. 'Why yes,' I reply, astounded. 'How did you know?' 'Because mothers of boys always walk — and talk — more confidently. I could hear it in your footstep and thought, she must have a son.'

The mother who confesses of her son, 'I don't know where he gets his brains from.' Oh, don't.

THE GIFT

Young children give so much and they don't even know it. The constant, soldering gift of them.

Never forget that kids watch us. And do as we do.

As parents we're teaching our children to wake up; to the wonder of the world, to its beauty.

Why is this enough for me now? Every night, a house filled with the sleep of my children and I have no desire to ever leave it. The love burns through me, the content.

'I could be more of a prison as an older, tense, cynical career girl than as a richly creative wife and mother who is always growing intellectually.'

SYLVIA PLATH

Twenty-two
CELIBACY

The demand
to live your own life...

'An essential freedom is the ability to say no.'

JEAN-PAUL SARTRE

Part I

A MAD AND SAVAGE MONSTER

The ebullience of women who are celibate by choice.

Power comes from sacrifices.

The devoutly single older women whose intellectual and emotional fulfilment is almost shocking. Their energy is channelled elsewhere. They're free, finally, and revelling in it.

Jerry Hall's wonder, post-Mick: 'It's amazing how much you get done when you're celibate.'

That time I was madly in love and existing in a golden morass of sex that seemed to slow me, kill my thinking. I got nothing done. I was living in the desert, and an Aboriginal elder said to me, 'I've become weak from pouring so much sugar into my tea.' It got me thinking. Can the pleasures of sex make you weak; interfere with your focus and calm?

The key is how you'd respond to the question: What if I never sleep with another man? With relief, or regret? And what you do about it.

Plato recorded, 'Someone asked Sophocles, "How is your sex-life now? Are you still able to have a woman?" He replied, "Hush, man; most gladly indeed am I rid of it all, as though I had escaped from a mad and savage master."

What if we were free? What then?

B., who expresses nothing but relief to be rid of sex. She's reclaimed her life through celibacy: 'I have myself back, Nikki.'

∞

Never forget the cleansing power of surprise.

∞

Part II

CELIBACY AND MOTHERHOOD

Lunch with the new mother who gave birth to a son four months previously. 'I just don't want [my husband] near me. When he kisses me, my whole body recoils. I don't understand because he used to really turn me on. It's like something's been extinguished; the pheromones or something. I keep on saying I'm too tired, too exhausted, but it's just that I can't stand the thought of having sex with him again. It's so strange. I'd be happy to be celibate for the rest of my life — except to make another baby.' She leans back in her chair. 'The weird thing is I get this almost-sexual satisfaction from being with my son. I love curling around him on the couch as he's asleep; holding him, touching him.'

I, too, have known something of what she says. My love for my little boys is weighty, voluptuous, it brims my life — and I know I am remiss as a wife. But it seems there was almost a biological urge within me, post-childbirth, to turn to the child and away from the father. The cruelty of nature. There was simply an immense feeling of being…sated.

Patrick White said that churches destroy the mystery of God — and I'd begun to believe that motherhood destroyed the mystery of sex. It was chipping away at my energy and my confidence. Suddenly I knew where Kafka was coming from: 'Coitus as punishment for the happiness of being together.'

The woman at the party who's not had sex with her partner for six years. She's in her late thirties and they've been together since she was twenty-two. 'I feel like just walking into a pub and finding some bloke — I'm ready to explode. I need sex.' She wants a baby. Her partner can't talk to her openly about why he has no sex drive. He's refused counselling, she wonders if he's gay. He's put on weight and she suspects that low self-esteem is a contributing factor. 'I don't care if he's a bit chubbier. We've settled into this weird brother/sister relationship — it's just…killing me.' She still loves him and can't bring herself to leave, even though she may never have a child.

Rupture is so often good, I gently suggest. 'What happens if you're in your late forties and still with him, and still not having sex? I think you'll be incredibly frustrated and bitter.' She sighs, turns her head, can't answer.

Part III

A LETTER

Dear Nikki,

    *I'm thirty-nine years old. I've been married for
eight years, but with a difference. I'm a virgin, and so
is my wife…*

This is the most intriguing letter I've ever received. I thanked
the correspondent for his courage in being so open with me,
and wasn't sure I'd ever hear from him again. I did.

    *…The trouble is, my mother was the only woman
I was ever comfortable with. My wife is the ideal
woman insofar as she reminds me of my mum in
terms of her qualities — but you don't sleep with
your mum, do you? And I'm shy, especially when it
comes to the nitty-gritty. When I met my wife I was
so thankful to find a woman who was interested in
me, I just grabbed her. How does she put up with it?
We have so much else in common, and we're both
comfortable with the situation now. Sex — or the
absence of it — doesn't seem a good enough reason
to leave.*

My friend, whatever works. And from the letters I've received from him it seems there's a lot of love in the relationship; love strengthened by a deep companionship and affection.

There's an acting exercise involving 'yes' sayers and 'no' sayers: people who say yes are rewarded by the adventure they go on, and people who say no are rewarded by their feeling of safety. And so these two people find comfort in safety. Sex, of course, can be incredibly bleak, lonely and ridiculous, ugly. A lot of literary big guns have lined up over the years to rubbish it. Take Evelyn Waugh for instance: 'All this fuss about sleeping together. For physical pleasure I'd sooner go to my dentist any day.' If it's not good sex, then why put yourself through it?

> *'Loyalty to petrified opinion never yet broke a chain or freed a human soul'*
>
> **MARK TWAIN**

You can feel chained by sex; fettered, disempowered, reduced. But if it works...well, there's nothing more life-affirming. There's something deeply spiritual about the best sex; there's a divinity to it. Sex is the most exhilarating mystery available to us. It can involve communicating with someone on the deepest level. We surprise ourselves — and our partners — with the level of our surrender. We strip ourselves bare. Apart from the obvious biological imperative, good sex flushes us clean and boosts our confidence — and freshens a partnership.

I'm haunted by this letter, for it seems a logical extension of Joseph Conrad's infinitely sad words, 'We live as we dream — alone.' But sex, great sex, defies that.

I left my mysterious correspondent with the French writer Colette: 'The day after that wedding night I found that a distance of a thousand miles, abyss and discovery and irremediable metamorphosis, separated me from the day before.'

'Go on, my friend, I dare you,' I wrote. 'Because I've always been on the side of the risk-takers.'

I never heard from him again.

Twenty-three
HONESTY

The clamour and deception of propaganda...

'I was taught bravery and that has influenced me.'

HELEN MIRREN

Part I

THE THERAPEUTIC BENEFITS
OF TELLING THE TRUTH

It's amazing how much support you get when you tell the truth.

How I admire those people who have the courage to not be like everyone else, but to be, simply, themselves.

'I have many reasons for believing that the truth purges one from fear. Many of us who, in recent years, strove to speak the truth in spite of everything were able to maintain an inner perspective, a willingness to endure, a sense of proportion, an ability to understand and forgive our neighbours, and a light heart only because we were speaking the truth. Otherwise, we might have perished from despair.'

VACLAV HAVEL

Part II

SECRET MEN'S BUSINESS

'I love shared sleep, even more so than sex, but I'd never tell a soul because it's not the male stereotype.' He wrote it furtively, embarrassed. If only he knew how much women would respond to his honesty.

That radio discussion involving five men and myself about sex, among other things. After the microphones were switched off the man sitting next to me said to no-one in particular, 'I hate getting blow jobs.' 'Me too,' another piped up. Pardon? Forty per cent of a group of men saying they don't like fellatio? 'Why didn't you say that on air?' I protested. 'It's the kind of thing women are really interested to hear.' Man number one glanced across calmly, straight in the eye: 'I didn't say it on air because I have a sexual stereotype to live up to.' My forehead sank to the table.

D. has never told his closest friends of his aversion to blow jobs: 'To admit it would mean you're a nerd. It's like telling your mates you don't drive well, or don't like footy.'

Others write that they prefer something else to sex, but find it hard to articulate. 'It's the closeness and intimacy I really need, not the sex,' P. wrote. 'Just sleeping beside her is something I love,' B. said. 'Being close, having her in my arms is such a joy, and all those men who say it's great being single and you can simply pick up a girl and shag her and then leave, well, they don't know what they're talking about.'

F.: 'Actually, I just want a cuddle a lot of the time.'

A letter from the other side: 'Nikki, I've just married for the third time to a "real man", who in private admits he's not very sexually motivated, but that a snuggle in bed and the security of knowing I love him is what turns him on. This usually results in our lovemaking. No man wants to admit that a cuddle turns them on, especially to his mates — and who am I to tell them otherwise? It's called love.'

'This above all: to thine own self be true.'

WILLIAM SHAKESPEARE

Part III

SECRET WOMEN'S BUSINESS

Women aren't allowed to be sexually vulnerable now — the men around us don't expect it of girls who grew up with *Cosmopolitan* magazine and had *Sex and the City* champagne nights. A lot of men assume that modern girls are much more accomplished, brazen and adventurous than a lot of us actually are.

'I was brought up for a girl who doesn't exist,' lamented my laddish neighbour in his twenties, as he threw out a pile of old *GQ* magazines.

When some of these women discovered their partners' deepest sexual desires, they were repulsed. 'Sex is the point of contact between man and nature, where morality and good intentions fall to primitive urges,' Camille Paglia wrote. It's glorious if the primitive urges are in harmony, but incredibly bleak if they're not.

'The whole business of eroticism is to destroy the self-contained character of the participators as they are in their normal lives,' Georges Bataille said. That's wonderful if both people involved are willing to be unmasked, to utterly surrender. But you're not going to find the grace and beauty in sex by being forced into a scenario you're uncomfortable with. Freedom means not having to participate in anything you don't like. I'm all for joyous experimentation — as long as both partners benefit. When only one does, what's the point?

The best experience is about mutual pleasure.

We're all at our most vulnerable when it comes to sex. It's the closest we get to revealing our true selves in all our banality, desperation and foolishness. The truly erotic isn't about perfection and accomplishment — it's about shedding our defences, fumbling, letting go. The intrigue lies in the glimpses behind the masks we all wear in public life. Sex tells the truth about us — it splits us open shamelessly and ruthlessly, reveals the core of who we are. If we surrender to it.

A lot of us can't face the thought of people seeing us as we really are, for it means losing control of the public persona we've so carefully maintained. And we never get closer to the truth of our dark, vulnerable, messy selves than with sex.

Are a lot of us women afraid of men seeing us as we really are? It helps to say exactly what we want — and where.

'One half of the world cannot understand
the pleasures of the other.'

JANE AUSTEN

art IV

WHAT REALLY WORKS
(OR WHAT WE'D REALLY LIKE, ACTUALLY, A LOT OF THE TIME)

What hints can we drop to our lover to create those legendary experiences that become soldered upon our memory? I began researching. Emailed girlfriends for help. Why exactly was their best-ever sex so amazing? What were those little touches that made it so incredible, the little lovelinesses we often never bother conveying to our partners? I wanted honesty above all. Curiously, not a single response made reference to the size of, erm, a certain male appendage.

Love came into it, a lot.

'The best sex I've ever had was the first time I realised I was in love with my boyfriend. It was at his place, a snuggly night in. Nothing special, just dinner and TV, but for some reason it all clicked and I realised I loved him. The sex was full of emotion.'

'It's with my husband. (I know, I'm so lucky!) He treats lovemaking with such a reverence; he only sleeps with someone he loves. And with that reverence comes a generosity of spirit — he won't ask me to do anything I don't like. There are moments of incredible tenderness.'

For a friend very much in the spotlight, her best experience came with the exhilaration of meeting a man who wasn't intimidated by her; of finally finding someone unafraid to love her.

For others, their best-ever sex hasn't always been with long-term partners:

'I was totally, physically into the guy. It was a brief, intense fling, and because I knew it wouldn't lead to anything long-term I found it incredibly liberating; I pushed back barriers that I'd never usually be brave enough to explore.'

Gentlemen, take note:

'He created a gorgeous atmosphere. His bedroom was like a cocoon: low music, soft lamps, candles. It was a wonderful nesting experience.'

'He held me as I came. He wrapped me in his arms and shared the experience.'

'He repeated my name over and over as he was climaxing. It was so…affirming.'

'He breathed close to my ear.'

'He holds back my hair as he kisses me deep.'

'He makes eye contact. It's such a simple thing but so lovely; reading his eyes as he's in me.'

'I love being rammed hard against a wall.'

'He's like a salt-sweeper after a dip in the surf — he mines my body with his lips and his tongue; he laps up the salt dried by the sun. It's really sexy.'

'I adore it when he falls asleep inside me; that he could feel so relaxed and...sated...with me.'

'She kisses my eyelids.'

'I love it when we burrow deep under the blankets on a cold Saturday night. It's often not about sex, but, to be perfectly honest, it's better!'

Twenty-four
WHEN LIFE IS CRUSHING

*I*ncrease, not hinder, morality…

*'...and life skips by like a field mouse
not shaking the grass.'*

EZRA POUND

Part I

HOW WELL WE HAVE LOVED

Years ago in New York I ran into a cathedral to escape a sudden thunderstorm. A priest, mid-sermon, was saying that at the end of our lives the question should be not what we have done, but how well we have loved. Oh yes.

The older I get, the more I respect kindness. Ditto generosity of spirit.

There are only two ways to live — the victim or the fighter. The fighter of courage and grace.

∞

Treat your enemy like your best friend.
Stun them, soften their heart.

∞

Remembering Mum's words, when T. betrays me: 'If you have one true friend you can forgive all the rest.' She's right. And I'm sure T. doesn't have any. Poor, spirit-emptied woman that she is. I also know that what she has done to me she has done to others. So many people warned me about her.

∞

It's strong people who have the courage to show their vulnerability.

∞

Part II

GETTING SOMETHING BACK

It's no use worrying about all the nasty things said about you because you only live once and life is to be enjoyed. Stop worrying, relax.

Part of growing up is admitting to who you are, and accepting it. Not being so hard on yourself.

People who have suffered are kinder, as if their edges have been softened by sorrow.

C.: 'Our shoulder blades are where our angel's wings once were.'

Remember that whatever you put out in life you get back. It is the great wondrous cycle of living.

∞

A life lived in fear is a life not fully lived.

∞

Old B.H. saying the one thing he has learnt in life is that you can only have happiness if you are a good person. As he talks, I contemplate the magnificent arc of happiness that is his life. He lives with gratitude; it is twinned with his goodness.

What nourishes the soul: Silence. Emptiness. Laughter. Nature. A child's joy. Rest.

'And the dark places be
Ablaze with love and poetry
When the power of good prevails.'

DEREK MAHON — 'AFTERLIVES'

art III

SINGLE MOTHERHOOD

K. has a son who's made it to Cambridge University, after being raised by her his whole life on a council estate. She's also got young twins. She's a wonderful mother, constantly reading to them and teaching them their letters, and they're the most beautiful kids. She knows, first-hand, the transformative power of education. It's the way out. Those children have her entire focus and they're benefiting gloriously from it.

J. and B. have both raised sons alone. Their boys have such a gentleness and confidence and a respect for women that's rare. It's enchanting to see.

There's often something...calm...in households with a lone matriarch. I find it myself when my A., God love him, is away on business. For then I'm doing things exactly my way — eating early with the kids, being extremely disciplined about bedtime and tidying up. No-one's telling me what to do, I'm in control and calling all the shots. And we all seem to benefit from the firm calm.

One thunderous commentator wrote that recent statistics on single parenthood had 'terrible social consequences in breeding poverty, underachievement and crime'. Well, they can also breed children determined to succeed in life and their own relationships. Thank God my parents didn't 'stick together for the kids' because the poisonous atmosphere, pre-divorce, was almost unbearable. Both my mother and father were a lot happier out of the marriage — and that resulted in happier kids.

And, I suspect, a more driven one.

'I'm not going to lie down and let trouble walk over me.'

ELLEN GLASGOW

'It is never too late to be what you might have been.'

GEORGE ELIOT

Part IV

FACING BREAST CANCER

T. says her sex life has improved since her breast cancer. I'm amazed to hear this from several women who've had it. 'I think it's because there's so much more honesty following the treatment; you can suddenly talk about anything,' explains my beloved R., who's also had a mastectomy. 'You're so much more honest about your body — and you're also more honest within your relationships.'

T. is a woman who seizes life; I can hear the spirit in her voice. Her advice for anyone facing a mastectomy: 'I think they should just see it as an experience to see how strong they can be. It's an achievement to get through.'

As for losing a nipple: 'Oooh, I don't mind at all,' she says. 'I've got another one! You just concentrate on the areas that work. And I told my doctor I'm still hoping to experience phantom nipple pleasure. What a delicious thought!'

Part V

FINDING YOUR GREAT GOOD PLACE

Henry James calls it 'a great good place' — a special place of calm and retreat and rest, just for you. We all have to have one.

When life is crushing, seek out the solace of the land. Night air fat with summer. The talking dark. Hurting light that floods your lungs and fills your bones. A canopy of stars. The hot white glare of a beach. The thump of the sea. Open your window wide to the land, let the enormous calm settle through you.

'There was nothing but land: not a country at all…
I had the feeling that the world was left behind,
that we had got over the edge of it.'

WILLA CATHER

∽

*Creativity nourishes us; it brings us
exhilaration and solace. We all need to nurture
our creativity — it's soul food.*

∽

Twenty-five
SWAN SONG

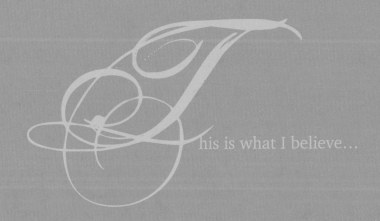

his is what I believe...

'To be nobody but yourself — in a world which is doing its best, night and day, to make you like everybody else — means to fight the hardest battle which any human being can fight; and never stop fighting.'

E.E. CUMMINGS

 ## To ALWAYS REMEMBER…

That a life driven by love is preferable to a
life driven by greed or ambition.

∞

That with sex, honesty is the most shocking
thing of all.

∞

That it's amazing how much support you
get when you tell the truth.

∞

That desire is a much more robust concept
than we sometimes give it credit for.

That it's wise to distance yourself from people who want to flatten you.

∞

That the most intense happiness can be found in the simplest of things: the sight of your father laughing uncontrollably during a film, a room filled with the sleep of your children, requited love.

∞

That a woman is sexy if she thinks she is.

∞

That shared sleep is deeply sexy; it's where true love lies, beyond words, beyond sex.

∞

That it's healthier in a relationship to be wanted rather than needed.

That there's not a person alive who doesn't want to be told they're loved.

∞

That as we age the wonder intensifies: do not retreat from it; the world is miraculous, so embrace it.

∞

That at the end of our lives the question should be not what we've done, but how well we've loved.

∞

'Life is only given us once, and one wants to live it boldly, with full consciousness and beauty.'

ANTON CHEKHOV

IN GRATITUDE

Thank you to all the glorious women around me (you heart-lifters you) for the wisdom, the solace and the laughs.

Thank you to my fabulously talented illustrator, Paula Sanz Caballero, for the gorgeous drawings.

Thank you to the entire Harper Collins Australia team for the dynamism, professionalism, energy and panache. Best in show!

Thank you to my endearingly eccentric London Library and its 'Women' section for the Victorian housewife manuals that provided inspiration for the chapter title pages.

Thank you to the Great Godwin.

Thank you to all the wonderful correspondents who've responded to my pleas for help, with both books and columns. I appreciate, so much, your knowledge, wit, understanding and honesty.

Thank you to the inspirational, good-hearted Sue Peart.

And thank you to Andy, Lachie and Ollie for making me laugh, so joyously, so much.

ACKNOWLEDGMENTS

Thank you to Tim Lott, Ian Marber, Derek Mahon, Les Murray, Alice Munro, Camille Paglia, Taki Theodoracopulos and the estate of Patrick White for allowing me to reproduce excerpts from their work.

Thank you also to the following: **George Bataille:** The extract from *Eroticism* is reproduced with the permission of Marion Boyars publishers. **Pearl S Buck**: The extract is from *The Patriot* with permission by Pearl S Buck c/– Harold Ober Associates. **E. E. Cummings:** Excerpt from 'A Poet's Advice to Students'. Copyright 1955, 1965 by the trustees for the E. E. Cummings Trust. Copyright 1958, 1965 by George J. Firmage, from *A Miscellany Revised* by E.E. Cummings, Edited by George J. Firmage. Used by permission of W.W. Norton and Company. **Robertson Davies:** Quote reprinted with the permission of Pendragon Ink. **Simone de Beauvoir:** The extract from *The Second Sex* is published by Jonathan Cape and reprinted with permission from The Random House Group Ltd. **Carol Ann Duffy:** The extract from the poem *Warming Her Pearls* is taken from *Selling Manhattan*, published by Anvil Press Poetry in1987. **Joseph Heller:** The excerpt from *Good as Gold*, published by Jonathan Cape, is reprinted with the permission of The Random House Group Ltd. **Sara Henderson:** The excerpt from *Outback Wisdom* is reprinted with the permission of Pan Macmillan Australia. **Rita Ann Higgins:** The excerpt is from *Throw in the Vowels: New and Selected Poems*, with the permission of Bloodaxe Books, 2005. **Ted Hughes:** The extract is from his introduction to *The Journals of Sylvia Plath*, published by Faber and Faber Ltd. **Edie Lederer:** Thanks to the author, Associated Press' chief correspondent at the United Nations and to Marquis *Who's Who in America*. **Pablo Neruda:** The extract from 'My Son' is taken from *Pablo Neruda: The Captain's Verses* translated by Brian Cole, published by Anvil Press Poetry, 1994. **Iris Murdoch:** The extract from *A World Child* is published by Chatto and Windus, reprinted by permission of The Random House Group Ltd. **Anais Nin:** Permission for these quotations is granted by Barbara W. Stuhlmann, Author's Representative. They are taken from *The Diary of Anais Nin, Volume Three.* **Ruth Pitter:** Extract from Ruth Pitter's Collected Poems (1996), published by Enitharmon Press, with permission. **Dodi Smith:** The extract from *I Capture the Castle*, published by Bodley Head, is reprinted by permission of the Random House Group Ltd. **Sylvia Plath**: The excerpt is from *The Journals of Sylvia Plath*, published by Faber and Faber Ltd. **Anne Sexton:** The excerpt from 'For My Lover, Returning to His Wife', is taken from *Love Poems*, Copyright (c) 1967, 1968, 1969 by Anne Sexton. Excerpt from 'Unknown Girl in the Maternity Ward' from *Bedlam and Part Way Back* Copyright 1960 by Anne Sexten, renewed 1988 by Linda G. Sexton. Reprinted by permission of the Houghton Mifflin Company. All rights reserved. **Evelyn Waugh**: The extract from *Vile Bodies* is reproduced by permission of Penguin Books Ltd. **Jeanette Winterson:** The extract from *Written on the Body* is reproduced by kind permission of the author, published by Jonathan Cape UK,1992. **Judith Wright:** The excerpt from "The Company of Lovers" is reproduced from *A Human Pattern: Selected Poems*, published by ETT Imprint, Sydney, 1996.

Every effort has been made to contact copyright holders. If there are any errors or ommissions we apologise to those concerend, and ask that they contact HarperCollins Australia so that we can correct any oversights as soon as possible.

Please note that some names, initials and circumstances have been changed.

*Take a deep breath — think of three
things to be thankful for — let the gratitude flow
through you — smile.*

*'A thankful heart is not only
the greatest virtue, but the parent
of all other virtues.'*

CICERO